Pacific Partners

Carin Holroyd and Ken Coates

James Lorimer & Company, Publishers,
Toronto, 1996

James Lorimer & Company Ltd. acknowledges with thanks the support of the Canada Council, the Ontario Arts Council and the Ontario Publishing Centre in the development of writing and publishing in Canada.

Canadian Cataloguing in Publication Data

Coates, Kenneth, 1956–
Pacific Partners

Includes index.
ISBN 1-55028-493-2 (bound)
ISBN 1-55028-492-4 (pbk.)

1. Canada — Commerce — Japan. 2. Japan — Commerce — Canada.
3. Canada — Relations — Japan. 4. Japan — Relations — Canada. I.
Holroyd, Carin. II. Title.

HF3228.J3C63 1996   382'.0971052   C95-933089-5

James Lorimer & Company Ltd., Publishers
35 Britain Street
Toronto, Ontario
M5A 1R7

Printed and bound in Canada

Contents

Acknowledgements

Pacific Partners represents an attempt to blend our very different backgrounds and interests—one of us being a Canadian historian and the other, a specialist in Japanese business. The struggle to educate each other has been, in many ways, the most delightful aspect of this project. That this book has appeared in print is the happy result of the contributions and assistance of many people. James Lorimer's enthusiasm for the project was a welcome beginning, and Diane Young's gentle, persistent and professional ministrations brought this book through many stages and several trials. James's and Diane's support and encouragement are greatly appreciated. We would also like to thank Eileen Koyama for her skilful copyedit of the manuscript and Laura Ellis for her careful proofreading. We also received considerable assistance and advice from friends and colleagues. We would like to thank, in particular, Klaus Pringsheim and Martin Thornell of the Canada-Japan Trade Council for their gracious assistance and advice. Ken Henshall, Chair of East Asian Studies at the University of Waikato examined portions of the manuscript and offered some extremely useful suggestions. Debby Zbarsky kindly read and commented on an early draft of the manuscript; her advice and encouragement came at a crucial moment and are greatly appreciated. Larry Woods of the International Studies Programme at the University of Northern British Columbia provided helpful advice. Greg Poelzer of the Political Science Programme at UNBC has been a great friend and an inspiration; his cheerful commentary and his willingness to listen to our many strange ideas helped push this project along. Ian Baskerville did a superb job of locating information and checking facts; his assistance with our research is greatly appreciated. These individuals bear no responsibility for the shortcomings of this book, but they certainly deserve a great deal of credit for its strengths.

In our research endeavours, we benefited greatly from the assistance of others. The Japanese Automobile Manufacturers Associa-

tion, the Council of Forest Industries of British Columbia, and numerous corporations were extremely gracious in providing information and answering our inquiries. This project capitalized, as well,
on the latest high-technology research tools, including the World
Wide Web site maintained by the Japanese Embassy for Canada (a
source of useful statistical information), and, in particular, the exter-
nally accessible databases operated by the Department of External
Affairs. We were helped in ways large and small by the wonderful
staff at the UNBC library. As well, this research project was assisted
financially by a grant in aid of research provided by UNBC.

This project stole precious time from friends and family. The
patience and understanding of Mark, Laura and Bradley Coates are
greatly appreciated; we hope that the publication of *Pacific Partners*
helps explain the constant heap of books on the dining room table.
Finally, we are very pleased to thank Beth and Les Holroyd for their
help, understanding, patience and compassion. The year in which this
book was written was exceptionally trying and, at times, painful.
That this book has been written is largely due to their graciousness
and caring. With thanks and with love, we dedicate this book to them.

Carin Holroyd and Ken Coates

Introduction

Canadian and Japanese baseball fans approach the game in radically different ways. Canadian devotees are, at best, unfocused. Thousands arrive late at their seats, preferring a prolonged wait in line at the concession counter for an obligatory beer to witnessing the first pitch. They spend much of their time in casual conversation, rarely connected to the game, and leave when the result has been settled (except in Toronto, where many leave at the end of the seventh inning, having made their "appearance" at what used to be the biggest show in town). The antics of a clownish mascot often elicit more of a reaction than a perfectly turned double play. The electronic scoreboard, with its regular commands to the crowd to cheer, clap, yell or otherwise show signs of life, is as much a part of the game as are the pitcher and catcher. Fans cheer as loudly about the frantic scrambling in the stands over a foul ball as they do about a strike out and pay greater attention to brawls in the cheap seats than to managerial options. Baseball remains a grand attraction, sustained, through a decade of escalating salaries, devastating strikes and the bizarre antics of owners and players, by the transformation of the night out at the ballpark into an entertainment extravaganza.

In Japan, fans go to the stadium to watch baseball. They follow the game with fanatical interest, their loyalty to the team and sport approximating that of the most devoted followers of the Montreal Canadiens hockey team. North Americans find a certain satisfaction—smugness, actually—in the fact that Japanese teams recruit a small number of foreign professional ball players, primarily Americans, Puerto Ricans and Koreans, to bring a higher level of skill and power to the Japanese game. (The prolonged strike in 1994 encouraged a number of big-name stars to throw in their financial lot with Japanese baseball teams.) The popularity of baseball is a classic illustration of the North Americanization of Japanese society, a sign that the established ways of Japan are surrendering to the crush of American popular culture.

North Americans would find numerous Japanese baseball rituals bizarre, if not unsettling. In Japan, the game is surrounded by rules and procedure. The fans focus intently on the on-field action and ignore distractions in the stands. The audience plays a vital role in the liturgy of baseball. Each player is greeted by an individualized chant as he approaches the batter's box. (There are Canadian equivalents, but they are generally reserved for star players, the occasional fan favourite or a hated opponent.) Proper decorum is followed throughout: managers do not kick dirt in anger, *à la* Billy Martin, or jaw face to face with an umpire. Bean balls are not tolerated; a pitcher is expected to apologize if he hits a batter accidentally, and the bench-clearing brawls that have become fan favourites in North America are unknown in Japan. And the fans stay to the very end; to do otherwise would be deemed impolite and even disloyal to the team.

Outsiders face special pressures and expectations. North American import players are expected to do well—but not too well. It is deemed best if Japanese players win most of the major awards, and the teams operate accordingly. For example, a team will walk an opposing import batter, even to its disadvantage, to prevent the hitter from challenging a home-run title. Import batters are expected to understand this approach. The Japanese make a distinction between "the inside and the outside." Those on the inside are part of a group, be it a family, a company, a team, a city, or Japan itself; those on the outside do not belong to this group. In baseball, the inside group is typically the home team, but when it comes to the performance of North American players, the inside group extends to cover all Japanese players. Hence, it is better for baseball if, in individual competitions, someone on the inside (i.e., a Japanese ball player) wins the major titles. The inside/outside relationship is not unique to professional baseball; rather, it permeates Japanese culture.

One should not make too much of the difference between home games of the Toronto Blue Jays and the Hanshin Tigers, for professional sporting events are not the perfect embodiment of any national culture. Still, fan behaviour at professional baseball games can be seen as a metaphor for the gap between the Canadian and Japanese cultures. Canadians, like baseball fans, lack singularity of purpose and emphasize individual behaviour, rather than collective participation. There is little intensity (save for those special autumn games in the pennant drive toward the World Series) and a preoccupation with the moment rather than the future.

In Japan, in sharp contrast, the individual is sublimated to the national or corporate good. Collective action and involvement is valued over personal initiative. The Japanese, like their baseball fans, approach major projects and issues with a focus and zeal that are rarely encountered in Canada. The overriding consideration is the long-term benefit for the nation or the collective, rather than short-term individual gratification.

These are sweeping generalizations and hence are subject to all of the flaws of oversimplification. But there is an essential element buried in the professional baseball metaphor. The analogy draws attention to the unique characteristics of Canada and Japan, and illustrates the cultural gulf between the two countries, a gap which may be broader than the ocean dividing them.

Stereotypes dominate each country's perceptions of the other. The Japanese are far more complex than the image generally held by Canadians implies: deferential, camera-toting, slavishly hard-working, fabulously rich as business investors, inscrutable, and conformist. Canadians, likewise, are more diverse than Japanese stereotypes would suggest, particularly since those images are primarily influenced by visions of Canadian wilderness, the *Anne of Green Gables* stories, a fascination with the Royal Canadian Mounted Police and a strong belief that the country is filled with loggers, miners and fishery workers. The language barrier renders the cultures more mysterious and impenetrable, adding to the complications and limiting the opportunity for mutual comprehension.

In this instance, as in most others, stereotypes are more than misleading—they are downright dangerous. In the past, Canadians reacted strongly to Japanese immigrants and Japanese Canadians largely on the basis of widely held misperceptions. The results, including racially motivated attacks and the evacuation of people of Japanese ancestry from the West Coast during World War II, were tragic indeed. More recently, Canadians have frequently misread Japanese business intentions, alternately fretting about the level of Japanese investment in the country and courting business leaders to contribute more yen to Canadian projects. The Japanese market has been held up frequently as an untapped treasure trove, offering untold riches to the first Canadian firms to capitalize on the obvious opportunities; it has also been derided as a government-protected oligopoly, fiercely devoted to Japan-first policies and resistant to international intrusions. The vacillating responses of Canadians to

Japan, and similar Japanese reactions to Canada, reveal the dangers of permitting misperceptions to persist unchallenged.

The underlying purpose of *Pacific Partners* is threefold. First, the book seeks to move beyond political statements, business fantasies and popularly held images to consider the true nature and extent of the Canada-Japan relationship. This association exists at a number of levels: historical contacts and issues, images of the other, political and diplomatic considerations, cultural and social understanding (and misunderstandings), and economic connections and opportunities. *Pacific Partners* deals with these topics in survey form, offering an overview and preliminary assessment, rather than a detailed analysis of these complex issues. The intention, then, is to offer an introduction to one of the most perplexing and potentially important bilateral relationships in the world, that between Asia and North America, an industrial superpower and an exporter of raw materials, a country seemingly at the economic pinnacle and another at the precipice of a serious decline, a monocultural state with strong connections to the past and a young, multicultural nation.

Second, the book explores the potential of Canada's relationship with Japan and encourages Canadians to think about what they would like that relationship to become. For decades, Canada has relied almost exclusively on the export of its raw materials and industrial products to the United States and has made little effort to seek other markets or develop new products. Japan, as the recipient of 4.5 per cent of Canadian exports, is Canada's second-largest export market (after the United States, which receives about 75 per cent!) and the third-largest investor in Canada (behind the United States and the United Kingdom). (Again, however, the difference in scale between the United States and Japan is staggering. In 1994, the United States invested $96 billion and Japan invested $5.8 billion in Canada.)

The rise in the value of the yen has caused changes in the Japanese economy, including a significant shift in its import profile to a much greater percentage of value-added products, an increase in investment in technology and further development of offshore labour-intensive manufacturing. Canada has paid little attention to these changes and has yet to decide as a nation the level of relationship it wishes to have with Japan. Many other nations are actively courting Japan's investment dollars and aggressively targeting its markets. If Canada does not make a decision and act, many of the opportunities will vanish.

Third, *Pacific Partners* tries to explore what Canada and Japan can learn from one another. Such different histories and cultures have naturally produced radically disparate nations facing unique challenges in the twenty-first century. There may be, however, important lessons for Canada in Japan's actions and national character. Karel van Wolferen, in his important book, *The Enigma of Japanese Power*, observes that in Japan "there is no supreme institution with ultimate policy-making jurisdiction. Hence there is no place where, as Harry Truman would have said, the buck stops. In Japan, the buck keeps circulating." Canada also lacks a definitive authority, and there is great uncertainty about who should be developing the country's economic plan or any other national strategy. The competing provincial and federal governments, combined with the cacophony of special-interest groups, have left Canada without true national leadership. While both Canada and Japan lack a "supreme institution" or guiding hand, the Japanese people are, for the most part, united "servants of the system," working for the good of Japan. Canadians, on the other hand, have been consumed by the demands of individuals, special-interest groups, provinces and regions.

Canada, much like Japan, is now fully entangled in the global community, competing for market share with nations around the world. The closed economic and cultural loops of the past (Canada with the United States and Britain; Japan with East Asia and, after World War II, the United States) are being replaced with complex and far-flung commercial relationships. Despite the changing nature of the economy, however, Canadians remain wedded to the world-view of the past, which placed unbending confidence in the continued demand for raw materials and on the inherent superiority of Western capitalist traditions. Canadians make few efforts to understand, let alone exploit, opportunities in other countries: consequently, Canada entered the era of global trade as a market weakling, lacking the vision, insight and ability to make the most of opportunities to preserve or expand international exchange.

In contrast, the Japanese took a radically different tack; they recognized the limited wealth of their natural resources and sought to capitalize on the country's greatest asset—people. They have made significant efforts to understand and thereby capitalize on the opportunities available in North America, although their image of the continent remains riddled with stereotypes (from America the violent to Canada the pristine). Just as the Japanese have often left Canadians behind in the development of industrial procedures, electronics and other manufacturing areas, Japanese business people have made the extra effort to learn our language and our ways of conducting business. It is clearly time—if only for the nation's self-interest—that Canadians make a concerted effort to move beyond the stereotypes about Japan and seek true understanding of the power, possibilities and difficulties in the Land of the Rising Sun. Japan is not the untouchable economic superpower it appeared to be only a few years ago; fraught with internal political difficulties, Japan faces a myriad of social and economic challenges and a potentially lengthy and painful period of readjustment. But with the second-largest economy in the world, Japan could still teach Canada something about teamwork and national purpose.

1

Canada and Japan Today

Vast distances separate Canada and Japan. Tokyo, 7,575 kilometres from Vancouver, is as far away as Lima, Beijing and Moscow. Toronto and Montreal, the Canadian centres of financial and political decision making, and Ottawa, the would-be focal point for Canadian policy making and authority, are over 10,000 kilometres from Japan. London, Paris, Rome and Stockholm are much closer than Tokyo to the central Canadian power triangle. If Canada and Japan are neighbours, they are distant neighbours indeed.

This is not to suggest that Canada and Japan have not been and are not connected, or that the two countries' destinies are not intricately intertwined. Indeed, the evidence of the past thirty years is convincing: Canada has come increasingly under Japan's economic sway, even though it still believes that the leaky American umbrella will be its commercial saviour. The relationship is without political or hegemonic overtones, despite Japan's evident economic clout and steadfast determination to preserve its position as one of the world's commercial leaders.

In sharp contrast to the Australians, whose reaction to massive Japanese investment in Queensland evoked historic images of Down-Under xenophobia, Canadians have paid relatively little attention to the mounting scale and character of Japanese economic involvement in their country. When a flurry of Hong Kong investment in the British Columbia housing market (aided by a much lower profile but very significant influx of capital and people from central Canada) sparked a sharp increase in house and land prices, local residents reacted angrily. While municipal and provincial politicians rushed to calm frayed nerves and soothe worried voters, tempers flared as yet more foreign investment was forcing up the price of the Canadian birthright—the single family home.

But compare this to the subdued response to massive Japanese investment in British Columbia coal, Alberta timber and central Canadian automobile manufacturing. In each instance, Japanese companies were welcomed as economic saviours, daring to invest where Canadian firms pulled back. If there was criticism, it focused largely on corporate control of key resources, potential environmental damage and the folly of massive government investments in megaprojects—not on the nationality of the investors.

And so, Canadian politicians, with the blessing of their constituents but typically with limited forethought or preparation, sporadically head off to Japan in an attempt to attract foreign investment and to thereby sustain the resource-based Canadian economy. Canadian emphasis on Japan as the second-choice saviour—the United States retaining first place—has waned lately, particularly following Prime Minister Jean Chrétien's much-touted tour of China in 1994. But many observers, without diminishing China's expanding role as an economic superpower, argue that Japan should figure prominently in Canada's plans for economic growth. Japan no longer arouses feelings of fear and loathing; it was not so long ago that the country and its citizens, and even Canadians of Japanese ancestry, evoked just such reactions. Now, more capitalist than the continent that redefined capitalism, more successful than any industrial power on earth, more commercially innovative than the continent that long prided itself on its capacity for creative adaptation, more hard-working than the continent that gave meaning to the "Protestant work ethic," Japan is viewed with a combination of envy, awe and resentment.

Japan, conversely, devotes little time and energy to coming to terms with Canada. While the Japanese are firm devotees of the United States and American culture—imitation is, after all, one of the country's great skills—they barely notice Canada and Canadians. There have been exceptions: megastar Bryan Adams and sprinter Ben Johnson (before the Olympic doping scandal). Lucy Maude Montgomery's *Anne of Green Gables* is extremely popular in Japan, as are the Royal Canadian Mounted Police (RCMP), the Rocky Mountains, Whistler Mountain and Niagara Falls. But to a country that considers the world to be its economic zone, major investments in Canada are but a tiny portion of its overseas exposure.

Canada is not insignificant: it ranks eighth in terms of the amount of trade goods brought into Japan. But many of the Canadian trade goods could be purchased from other countries, often at better prices. It is Canada's solidity, its political and economic stability, that is most attractive to Japan, a country with a fierce concern about long-term supplies of raw materials. And so, while Canadian political and commercial leaders fret about economic ties to Japan, Japan devotes comparatively little effort to worrying about Canada.

Lack of interest aside, Japan has established a considerable presence in Canada, being second only to the United States in terms of economic importance. The recent Japanese expansion of the Toyota plant in Cambridge, Ontario was undertaken to capitalize on a well-trained labour force and, under the terms of the North American Free Trade Agreement (NAFTA), on Canadian access to American markets. The massive investment, totalling $600 million, was hailed by Canadian politicians as evidence of the country's continued attractiveness and of the long-term benefits attached to the free trade deal. Similarly, Japanese investments in two northern Albertan pulp mills generated hundreds of short-term construction jobs and revitalized the logging industry in the northern half of the province. The ubiquitous Japanese tourist—closely shepherded among tour bus, hotel, scenic vista and retail store with Japanese-speaking clerks—has also become an increasingly important part of the economic equation. Canadian and Japanese authorities recently announced a joint effort to substantially increase Japanese tourism to Canada (as part of an ongoing Japanese effort to dampen international concern about Japanese trade surpluses by participating in cooperative ventures).

Canada is much further down the line in Japan's commercial hierarchy, a comparatively small player in the hotly contested world of international trade. Raw materials continue to make up the bulk of Canada's trade with Japan, as they did before World War II, and it is considered a major achievement when any Canadian processed goods find a niche in the Japanese market. Some are starting to do so, although typically with strong assistance from Japanese firms. Mitsui Homes, the largest seller of prefabricated two-by-four homes in Japan, has long purchased many of its wood products from British Columbia. In 1994, the company established a prefabricating plant in the Lower Mainland, thus permitting Canadian industry (albeit Japanese-owned) to capture a portion of the value-added wood products trade. In most areas, Canada faces direct competition from suppliers in Australia, New Zealand, Indonesia and Chile, among others. Creating and holding a niche in the resource sector is proving to be increasingly difficult and represents an ongoing challenge for the Canadian business and exporting sectors.

Commercial ties do not, of necessity, create cultural links, and the gap between Canada and Japan in this area remains substantial. Canadians know very little about Japan (Grade 6 students in British

Columbia study Japan, but the country shares equal billing with Peru and Egypt), and have limited access to images and information about Japanese culture. Major events, such as the Kobe earthquake and the Tokyo terrorist attack, receive the same kind of media "McCoverage" that has sanitized cultures worldwide, offering superficiality where depth is required. Japanese movies show up at only the most avant-garde film festivals, which is probably more often than Canadian films are seen by Japanese audiences. Both countries wallow in the excesses of American popular culture, and both worry about sustaining their cultures in the face of the draining and demoralizing influences of international media.

What Canadians and Japanese offer each other is politeness and cordiality. The two countries have many sister-city arrangements, several of which are active and mutually beneficial. Canadians are enthusiastic participants at Japanese world and international fairs, and Japan always participates in Canadian extravaganzas, such as Expo '86 in Vancouver. Student exchanges are now commonplace, although the flow from Japan to Canada (to study English) is much greater than that in the opposite direction. Although there are relatively few Japanese language courses in Canada, this situation is changing, and many courses at the secondary and postsecondary level are now available, particularly in British Columbia. Japan, in contrast, requires that all students study English (not because of Canadian connections, one hastens to add), albeit of a peculiarly Japanese sort. Exchanges run by non-profit and private business organizations abound, particularly those sending Japanese students to Canada. Both national governments support a variety of cultural, academic and commercial exchanges and linkages, such as the university-based Japanese Association for Canadian Studies and the Japan Studies Association of Canada, but in much the same desultory fashion that they encourage other international and cross-cultural connections.

Canada and Japan Compared

There are few countries more dissimilar than Canada and Japan. Canada is large (997,614,000 hectares), thinly populated (30 million people), ethnically diverse, and marked by distinctive regional cultures, the most notable of which are the Québécois and the First Nations. Japan is very small (37,780,000 hectares) and densely populated (125 million), with a rare degree of ethnic homogeneity— 99.1 per cent Japanese. The dominant languages (English and French in

Canada, Japanese in Japan) bear no resemblance to each other, and residents in both countries have great difficulty learning to converse in the other's language. Canada's largest city, Toronto, has 3.8 million people; Tokyo, the dominant centre in Japan, is home to over 20 million residents.

Japan, a series of rocky islands in the North Pacific, stretches 2,170 kilometres from north to south at roughly the same latitudes as the area between Montreal and Miami. Okinawa, a territorial protectorate until 1972, when it was formally made part of Japan, is only 650 kilometres from Taiwan; Hokkaido, the northernmost island (save for the contested Kuril Islands, currently occupied by Russia), is only 400 kilometres from the Russian mainland. As the 1995 Kobe earthquake demonstrated with devastating effect, the Japanese archipelago is highly vulnerable to earthquakes; it is also part of the Pacific Rim volcanic zone. The Japanese climate is comparatively benign. The mountains and the north island do get snow but do not become exceedingly cold; Okinawa is subtropical.

Canada is the world's second-largest country, stretching 5,514 kilometres from east to west and 4,634 kilometres from north to south. The halfway point, measured north to south, is actually north of Yellowknife in the Northwest Territories, a simple fact that highlights Canada's basic northernness. The country is dominated by the Canadian Shield, a vast, rocky, lake-filled sweep of land that extends from Labrador to the Northwest Territories. Massive mountain ranges, the Coastal, Selkirk and Rocky Mountains, dominate the westernmost province of British Columbia; to the east, the expansive northern extension of the Great Plains covers much of Alberta, Saskatchewan and Manitoba. The older mountains of Ontario and Quebec lack the drama and sharpness of the western peaks, but they shield the rich agricultural lands of the Great Lakes–St. Lawrence lowlands. And further east lie the picturesque coastal lands of the Maritime provinces and Newfoundland, their beauty masking a scarcity of marketable resources, particularly since decades of overfishing have plundered the previously cod-rich waters of the Grand Banks.

The country is defined, internally and internationally, as much by its weather as by its geography. The cold winters are the country's signature, celebrated in art and culture, but resented by a southern-facing nation. Canadians huddle close to the Canada–United States border. Despite the rhetoric of being a northern nation, over half of the Canadian population lives south of the forty-ninth parallel (the boundary between western Canada and the western United States) and over 90 per cent of all Canadians live within 300 kilometres of the Canada–United States border. The vast northern expanses of the country, providing much of Canada's resource wealth, remain sparsely populated with extremely transient nonaboriginal populations.

Canada's economy is still based on two central elements: resource development with primary processing and manufacturing for the American market. This dependent, comparatively stagnant economy now follows the peaks and valleys of American economic performance with distressing regularity. In contrast, Japan has had one of the world's strongest, most creative and most internationally complex economies since the miraculous postwar recovery. Eight of the world's ten largest banks are Japanese, and large Japanese corporations rank among the most influential in the world. Canada, in contrast, has only a minor international presence, and it is dominated by foreign-owned corporations operating branch plants or, since NAFTA, using Canada as a base for selling into the American market. While Canada's economic fortunes remain substantially tied to forest products, minerals, oil and gas, and agricultural produce, Japan boasts the world's most dynamic industrial establishment, but has virtually no raw materials, making it by necessity an international trading nation.

The countries also bear little cultural resemblance to each other. Japan is uniquely homogeneous: it is overwhelmingly, enthusiastically Japanese, denying benefits to immigrants (including the hundreds of thousands of second- and third-generation Koreans in the country) and making few accommodations for cultural differences. Newcomers are expected to conform to Japanese customs and traditions, but are not readily accepted into the mainstream. Canada, conversely, operates around an official celebration of diversity and multiculturalism. While there are cracks in the facade of cultural understanding—occasional outbreaks of racism against East Indians in the West, Caribbean immigrants in the East—the country has a unique record of welcoming newcomers and integrating them into Canadian society.

Japan and Canada are so different—physically, culturally, linguistically, economically and politically—that it is hardly surprising that their relationship is not closer. When the not-yet-forgotten legacy of World War II is thrown into the equation, along with Canada's historical antipathy to the immigration of Asians, the explanation for a gap greater than the North Pacific becomes self-evident. But the most fascinating element to this story is that, predating World War II, Canada and Japan have remarkably good relations, belying the geographic, social and historical realities. Japan was the third country, following Britain and the United States, to host a Canadian consulate. And over the past thirty years, this formal contact has been followed by economic integration and increasing trade.

Japanese Involvement in Canada: A Case Study

On the surface, northern British Columbia shows few signs of interest in, let alone connection to, Japan. Unlike Banff, Jasper, Vancouver, Victoria and Whistler, where the influx of Japanese tourists has spawned a proliferation of commercial signs and retail services in Japanese, northern British Columbia shows little public accommodation of the Japanese. Japanese tourists, who prefer packaged holidays to the more free-form adventures available in this district, have generally stayed away. This is, on the surface, one part of the country that has not yet developed strong interest in Japan.

But in northern British Columbia, as elsewhere in the country, scratching below the surface reveals a different picture. The regional economy has numerous direct and indirect ties to Japan. One of the world's largest aluminum smelters, Alcan's Kitimat Works, sells 60 per cent of its production to Japan and retooled its plant specifically to serve this market. The largest resource development in the region in the past twenty years is the Northeast Coal Project, which is centred in Tumbler Ridge and has rail connections to a newly built coal terminal in Prince Rupert. It was designed entirely to service Japanese industry. Japanese companies own 50 per cent of the two pulp mills in Quesnel, the largest employers in this community of 9,000 people. On the northwest coast, close to 90 per cent of all fish and ocean products are shipped directly to Japan. Further north, in Fort Nelson, sits the world's largest chopstick factory, which is owned by a Japanese company and which sells to the Japanese. On a more exotic level, the annual, unregulated and frenzied pine mushroom harvest in the Terrace region owes its origins and viability to Japanese trade. And the north's vibrant lumber industry has numerous, important connections to the Japanese market.

The economic connections, which account for a surprising portion of the region's economic activity, have not yet been matched by social and cultural links. But the bonds are developing: sister-city connections between Quesnel and Shiraoi, and Prince Rupert and

Owase; Japanese language instruction in one of Prince George's high schools; English immersion programs for Japanese students at Northern Lights Community College; an emphasis on Japan and the Pacific Rim at the new University of Northern British Columbia; and a variety of school and community exchange programs. In spite of these developments, the regional newspapers pay no special attention to Japanese affairs, even those economic factors which might well have a direct and dramatic impact on northern British Columbia.

The same is true across the Pacific. The Japanese show no special interest in northern British Columbia, which is only one of hundreds of areas around the world where Japanese corporations have made major investments. Northern British Columbia is not even unique, competing for coal contracts with Australia, for lumber market share with New Zealand, and for investment dollars with cities and regions around the globe. But the Japanese, by the sheer weight of their economic power and the targeted nature of their investments, have taken on a vital role in northern British Columbia and, indeed, across Canada. It is a role that few Canadians have identified and fewer corporations have fully exploited.

Northern British Columbia is but one example of many regions in Canada in which Japan has established a major presence. Through its direct investments and purchases in these areas, Japan is now instrumental in influencing Canada's economic prospects. Meanwhile, Canadians are justifiably preoccupied with American political and economic developments, and continue to offer only an occasional passing glance at their mysterious, second-largest trading partner. Northern British Columbia has been profoundly affected by Japanese commercial involvement, just as all of Canada has felt the impact of Japanese trade, but the region remains surprisingly uninterested in learning more about the country that plays such a pivotal role in its economic and social future. Greater knowledge—of the historic and contemporary relationships, of the barriers and opportunities, of cultural differences and political influences—is necessary to capitalize fully on the potential of the Canada-Japan relationship.

As a starting point, it is worth considering the contemporary situation in Japan. Canadians generally receive only snippets of information about news events in Japan—a terrorist gas attack on Tokyo subways, the Kobe earthquake, unusual business developments, changes in the Nissan industrial empire (the Japanese have access to even less news about Canada, for the country tends to break into the international newscasts only when there is a scandal or when the spectre of Quebec separation does its regular dance). While North Americans have the general impression that the lustre of the Japanese economic marvel has faded, and a limited understanding of the on-going political turmoil in the country, most Canadians know very little about the lengthy recession, the changing demography, the legacy of political radicalism and the shifting internal industrial landscape. The Japan of the late 1990s is not the Japan of the mid-1980s and is far removed from the country that pushed its way onto the world economic stage in the 1960s.

Japan's Challenges

The Japanese can be both incredibly confident and deeply insecure, continually swinging between a sense of assumed superiority and feelings of inferiority in their dealings with other nations. They spent decades trying to catch up with the West and win its approval, but at the same time a sense of distinctiveness and divine descendance seems to permeate their thinking. There is, in fact, a veritable intellectual industry that flourishes around the study of what—biology, heredity, history or culture—makes Japan unique. The roaring economic successes of the postwar era, which both reflected and reinforced the population's commitment to national goals, attitudes and values, convinced the Japanese that the loss of World War II in no way marked the end of Japanese confidence and the country's importance. (Not incidentally, revisionist novels about the war, featuring Japanese victories in battles lost and presenting scenarios about the invasion of North America, are enjoying a brisk market at present.)

But even the country of the economic "miracle" has serious internal difficulties. Some of these problems are currently being played out on the world stage; others are little known outside of Japan. Together, they reflect a society in the midst of a potentially traumatic evolution that could recast the core values of Japanese life and that points out the cracks in the facade of modern Japanese invulnerability. Of these, the following are particularly worthy of notice:

Political Instability:

In the last few years, Japan has been shaken by a variety of tensions and struggles. In July 1993, the Liberal Democratic Party (LDP) lost its majority in the House of Representatives for the first time in thirty-eight years. Financial scandals and the politicians' reluctance to enact political reforms have frustrated and disillusioned the Japanese electorate. In the two years that followed, the Diet has been run by coalition governments characterized by continued jockeying for power and position. In roughly six years, Japan went through seven prime ministers, a record rivalling that of Italy, one of the world's most notoriously unstable democracies.

Social Instability:

The Japanese have long prided themselves on being one of the safest developed nations, known globally for a high level of social cohesion, a low rate of crime and a commitment to order. Recent events have shocked and horrified the nation, and thrown the country's basic stability into question. In March 1995, a nerve-gas attack on Tokyo's subways killed twelve people and poisoned 5,000. Ten days after the Tokyo incident, a masked gunman seriously wounded the director-general of the National Police Force. The next month, a different kind of gas was released at Yokohama's main train station, sending over 500 people to hospital. Two days later, yet another attack at a Yokohama shopping centre resulted in twenty-five people being hospitalized. Arrests have now been made in the gas attacks, and the cases are expected to move swiftly through the courts.

The public and the police are also nervous about changes within the *yakuza*, Japan's underworld. Until recently, the *yakuza* concentrated on protection rackets, gambling, prostitution and related illegal business. They did not carry guns, deal in narcotics or harm innocent citizens. In the boom years of the 1980s, gangsters began to work their way into legitimate businesses by speculating on stocks and property. When the boom ended, causing bankruptcies and soaring bad debts, the *yakuza* brought terror into the mainstream business world. At least three Japanese executives have been shot in what police suspect are *yakuza* killings, and a number of other executives are currently under police protection. The underworld is becoming more violent, more unpredictable and more frightening.

The increase in foreign workers in Japan, the changing role of women and the rapidly aging population (experts estimate there will be 21 million seniors by the year 2000) have the potential to disrupt a country that places a premium on harmony and cohesiveness.

Role on the World Stage:

Japan has long preferred to play a somewhat understated role internationally. Article 9 of the Japanese Constitution states the country's renunciation of war and has allowed Japan to limit its military activities (although it still has the world's sixth biggest armed force), shunning participation even in peacekeeping missions until very recently. When war broke out in the Persian Gulf in 1992, Japan chose to contribute money to the effort but did not send troops; it was roundly criticized internationally for that decision. Japan is under increasing pressure to play a stronger role, not just militarily, in world affairs. Its strong economic standing has put it in the position of being a leader; other nations wish it to behave like one.

Remembering World War II:

Memories of Japan's behaviour before and during World War II remain firmly etched in the minds of many East Asians. Japanese investment and aid monies are helping to heal some of these wounds, but Japan still has a long way to go to overcome the animosity that exists against it in Asia. Japan has traditionally avoided making direct apologies to war victims or even teaching its youth about the atrocities committed during the war. This selective rendering of the past has served to anger the victims even more. In August 1995, on the occasion of the fiftieth anniversary of the end of World War II, Japan's prime minister broke with the past and offered something very close to an apology to the victims of his country's military aggression. That this apology, which came from the cabinet and not from Parliament, was so hotly debated within the country illustrates that the memory of World War II remains a delicate issue in Japan.

Education System:

Japan's education system has much about which it should be proud. All Japanese children graduate from junior high school and over 90 per cent complete senior high school. Despite the complexity of the written language, 99 per cent of the population is functionally literate, giving Japan one of the highest literacy rates in the world. On international math and science tests, Japanese children tend to rank first. There are more universities in Japan than in the whole of western Europe, and Japan produces twice as many engineers per capita as does the United States. Where the system falls short, however, is in its ability to produce creative, innovative, problem solvers. Children who are different or who express their individuality do not fit well into the Japanese system. Schoolyard bullying and teenage suicides are increasing, as is concern about the intense pressure on students to succeed within the school system. Japanese pupils are trained to take tests and memorize facts. They are not taught to ask

questions, express opinions, write essays or think for themselves—
key abilities if the country is to fulfil its role as a world leader.

Housing:

In Japan's large urban centres, the lack of space and affordable
housing is becoming an increasing problem. An apartment within the
Yamanote subway line, which forms a large circle in central Tokyo,
is purported to fetch the same price as an entire apartment block in
Hokkaido. Sociologists have begun to argue that Japanese society,
once famed for its enormous middle class, will be divided into two
categories in the future: those who own property and those who do
not. Some anxious home purchasers are signing 100-year mortgages,
thus ensuring that the next generation inherits part of a home and a
healthy mortgage. Crowding and the absence of good, affordable
housing are becoming pressing issues throughout the country, but
particularly in the Kanto region.

Trade Imbalances:

Despite the continued rise in the value of the yen (until very recently), Japan has generally enjoyed very favourable balance of trade
accounts with its partners, and for many years has had the largest
trade surplus in the world. Its balance of trade with the United States
in particular has been greatly in its favour. The Americans have been
pressuring Japan to take dramatic domestic action to correct the
situation, and recent trade conflicts have come close to creating a
serious breach between the world's two largest economies. Japan has
been liberalizing its markets and increasing its investments in offshore manufacturing facilities and seems intent on continuing to do
so, but it is not moving at the speed or to the extent desired by the
United States. The absence of a firm hand at the nation's helm
reduces the possibility of strong initiatives. There is talk of the
country heading into a recession or having to make sweeping changes
to its import and business regulations in an effort to stabilize the
value of its currency, which has dropped considerably from postwar
peaks.

Japan faces other problems. It must cope with the aftermath of the
Kobe earthquake and respond to environmental challenges, the
changing relationship between government and business, the growing restlessness of Japanese youth, an emerging generational gap
largely related to work habits, and international criticism of its whale

and dolphin harvests. Just as the image of the Japanese miracle was too good to be true, so it is incorrect to suggest that Japan stands poised on the precipice of internal chaos and social unrest. Japan will likely emerge from its current economic difficulties in a strong fashion, and the appearance of elements of social and political dissension does not presage a collapse of the cohesion that has held the country together through more difficult times than these. At the risk of stating the obvious, however, the Japan of the early twenty-first century will not be the Japan of the 1980s or even the 1990s.

***

The next decade will prove pivotal for both Canada and Japan. The verities of the 1960s and 1970s gave way to the uncertainties of the 1980s and the dramatic transitions of the 1990s. Both countries face uncertainty, if only because the operations of the world economy are now so interdependent and unpredictable. However, it is clear that Canada-Japan relations are strong and vital, and that, while they are more important to Canada than to Japan, they offer excellent benefits to each nation. A great deal has been left fallow; Canadians have made only a limited effort to come to terms with Japanese language and culture, whereas the Japanese are relatively well versed in the aspirations of North Americans and their ways of life. Overall, both sides have made little effort to capitalize on the potential of the relationship.

The mystique of resource wealth gives Canadians a false sense of security. While an abundance of wood, coal, minerals and foodstuffs has enabled Canada to forge strong trade links with Japan, Japan's needs are changing, and Canada's edge is slipping. Japan, conversely, has benefited from establishing industrial plants in Canada, with Canadians giving little thought to the long-term implications of these investments. A sizeable portion of Canada's resource wealth has long been controlled by outsiders—the British and then the Americans—so the pattern is familiar. In an increasingly globalized economy, where control of scarce resources is a desirable advantage, Canada's willing surrender of these resources to corporations structured to benefit another country may not be wise. Canadian images of hewing wood and drawing water have always been vaguely romantic and have strengthened and informed the national mystique; but they do not benefit Canada in times of high-technology industrialization and mass computerization. Japan has done nothing but play by the rules that Canada has set; Canadians may, as time unfolds, prove to be the architects of their own misfortune.

In the late 1990s, Canada and Japan are good friends, solid trading partners and international allies. Their economies are closely linked. Language and culture, more than physical distance, have kept the countries apart and have prevented commercial interaction from creating the foundation for greater mutual understanding. For generations, Canadians have surrendered a portion of their sovereignty to international corporations and, more recently, financial institutions; Japan, in contrast, has used its miraculous economic expansion as the base for gaining economic and indirect political influence on a global scale. Canada has become something of a good-natured dolphin, swimming alongside the massive, sleek and impressive Japanese ship: pleasant enough company, sustained by the small leavings of the richer country and blissfully unaware of the unrealized potential that lies within this important relationship.

2

Distant Neighbours: Canada and Japan to the 1930s

Canada and Japan occupied different worlds, found their spiritual inspiration in different deities and developed along strikingly dissimilar social, cultural and economic lines. Perhaps most significant, they knew and cared very little about the other. If Canada and Japan were neighbours before the second half of the twentieth century, they were akin to neighbours who had the Grand Canyon or the Rocky Mountains between their homes. Connected by an ocean that neither travelled extensively, Canada and Japan wove vastly different strands of the historical and cultural tapestry that would, over many generations, emerge to form the modern world.

Save for a small number of historical circumstances—Canada's flirtation with the "Silk Trains" to the Orient in the late nineteenth century and the Pacific War of 1941 to 1945—the Pacific Ocean figured only minimally in the evolving relationship between Canada and Japan. The Pacific existed, alternately, as an impenetrable barrier that divided continents and kept peoples far apart or as a trade route for the commercial operators who created and then exploited opportunities across the vast, widely differentiated, and ill-connected region. However, the passage of large numbers of sailing ships, cargo vessels and, more recently, airplanes does not necessarily make a region and does not necessarily create a deep and intense relationship.

The separate development of the two countries is an important element in their subsequent relations. Canada was created, following the commencement of western exploration, by contests between European nations. Japan, in contrast, resisted the incursions of outsiders, and established successful bulwarks against cultural, political and technological invasions by the European powers that had successfully partitioned much of the rest of the world. The distinctiveness of Japan, then, emerged by design rather than by historical happenstance, a fact that plays a pivotal role in explaining Japan's twentieth-century relations with the Western world. However, the two countries did not remain completely apart. The arrival of Japanese migrants to Canada, primarily to British Columbia, brought Japan to Canada, sparking a nativistic reaction among the population and, over time, straining relations between the nations. An overview of the history of Japan provides a brief but vital glimpse into the forces that shaped the country's history and established the foundation for Japan's belated contact with the Western world.

The Roots of the Japanese Nation

Japan has a burning historical consciousness, a powerful sense of place and purpose and a solid understanding of its shared values and customs. The country is deeply rooted in the past, its history conditioning Japan's twentieth-century development. If Canada can be characterized as a country in search of a history, and one largely adrift from shared values and traditions, Japan is best understood as a nation dominated by its historic evolution.

According to Japanese mythology, the islands of Japan were formed when a god and goddess, Izanagi and Izanami, leaned down from heaven and stirred the ocean with a jewelled spear. When they lifted the spear out of the water, the first island was created from drops of sea water, and the heavenly couple descended to earth. It is said that the sun goddess, Amaterasu, was then created out of a bronze mirror held in Izanagi's left hand.

Amaterasu, the story goes, was upset with the antics of her brother, Susanō, and hid herself in a cave, thereby plunging the world into darkness. Using a sword, some jewelled beads and a mirror, the other gods in the heavens laughed and danced about, in hopes of enticing Amaterasu out of the cave. Amaterasu became entranced by her vision in the mirror. As soon as she came out of the cave to get a closer look, the other gods slammed the cave door behind her, allowing sunlight to reach the earth.

Later, Amaterasu's grandson was sent down to earth to become the first emperor of Japan. All Japanese emperors are believed to be descended from him. Before her grandson left, Amaterasu gave him three gifts: a bronze mirror, a sword and a curved jewel. These now form the Japanese Imperial Regalia.

Beyond the mythological accounts of Japan's origins, the country has a long and storied past, which established the core values and social structure of contemporary Japan. Several crucial developments took place during the Tokugawa era (1600–1868). The leaders of this period went to great lengths to ensure the stability and survival of the regime. Potentially disloyal *daimyo* (feudal lords) were given territory in remote parts of the country or were given domains surrounded by lands held by loyal *daimyo*. All *daimyo* were obliged to annually alternate their residence between their domain and Edo. When the lords were in Edo, the Shogun could keep an eye on them and when they returned to their homes, their families were left behind as hostages. Maintaining two residences and travelling back and forth, often with hundreds of retainers, was an expensive proposition and ensured that the *daimyo* were unable to amass much wealth. These arrangements hastened the construction of a network of roads across the country, creating a transportation system that later proved vital for trade and commerce.

The Tokugawa leaders also sought to isolate Japan from contact with the outside world. They feared that some of the more powerful lords could increase their military and economic might if allowed to trade with foreigners. They banned all contact with outsiders. Trade was limited to a small Dutch trading post on Deshima Island in Nagasaki harbour and some very limited contacts with China and Korea. Christians were persecuted and forced to recant; missionaries were expelled. In 1636, overseas Japanese were prohibited from returning to Japan for fear that they might reintroduce Christianity. By 1638, Christianity had been virtually eliminated. Japanese ships were limited to those unsuited for ocean voyages and all Japanese were prohibited from travelling abroad.

Thus, for two centuries, while other non-European nations were experiencing the ravages of colonization and the massive changes that accompanied the introduction of new technology, Japan shut itself off from the rest of the world and developed in almost complete isolation. The Tokugawa era was a time of peace and stability. During this period, Japan's strong sense of national identity grew, its rich cultural heritage developed and the economy flourished.

The Tokugawan society was feudal in nature and was made up of four classes: warriors or samurai, peasants, artisans and merchants. The merchants were deemed to be the lowest class in society because their role was perceived to be more parasitic than productive. However, as the decades passed, the samurai became more and more financially indebted to the merchants. Over the same period of time, the warrior class underwent some changes. At the onset of the Tokugawa era, the samurai was a fighting class, but two and a half centuries of peace meant that, although the samurai still wore swords, they had essentially become government bureaucrats.

The Tokugawa system might well have continued for longer had it not been for the arrival of foreigners. Although Japan wished to maintain its isolation, various Western nations pressured Japan to open its doors. They wanted safe harbours for their ships, when they sailed past in search of whales or on their way to China. They also wanted access to Japan's markets. There were a number of Western attempts to induce Japan to end its isolation, but all were rebuffed. Finally, in 1853, the United States sent roughly one-quarter of its navy under Commodore Matthew Perry to force Japan to open its ports to American ships. These *black ships*, so-called by the Japanese for the clouds of black smoke emitted by these steam-powered vessels, contained enough cannon power to destroy Edo (today's Tokyo). The Japanese recognized their vulnerability, and in 1854 they signed a treaty that opened two ports for ships seeking provisions, guaranteed that shipwrecked sailors would receive good treatment and permitted the United States to send a consul to Japan. The task of negotiating the first trade agreement (signed in 1858) fell to this first consul, Townsend Harris. Treaties with the Dutch, Russians, British and French followed soon after.

These sudden changes caused great political, economic and emotional disruptions for Japan. Popular feelings ran strongly against the opening of the country. When faced with Perry's demands, the Edo government had asked for both the support of the *daimyo* and the emperor's approval, but had received neither. The government, therefore, had left itself open to a barrage of criticism. Many people felt that, to deal with these foreigners effectively, they would need to rally around the emperor in a show of unity and nationalism. Their rallying cry became Sonnō Joi (Revere the Emperor, Expel the Barbarians). Others were determined to learn from the West, even if only to use that knowledge to beat the Westerners. Samurai from all over the county discussed and debated Japan's options.

In some of the larger territories, the samurai openly disagreed with Edo's decisions and challenged the government's authority. Finally, in 1868, a coalition of samurai from Choshu, Satsuma and some of the other outer domains seized control of the imperial court and announced the resumption of imperial rule. The emperor would now be at the centre of the political system, giving it legitimacy and authority. (This did not mean, however, that real power would rest with the emperor any more than it had in the past.) The sixteen-year-old Emperor Meiji was moved from Kyoto to Edo and settled into the great castle of the shogunate. Edo was renamed Tokyo (eastern capital), and the whole transformation became known as the Meiji Restoration.

Meiji and Modernization

The Meiji era in Japan is synonymous with modernization and the country's entry into the industrial world. From 1868 to 1912, the Meiji Restoration witnessed the lightning transformation of Japan, and its emergence as a major world power. The young emperor held the seat of power, but a number of young samurai, primarily from Satsuma and Choshu, were the true leaders of the Meiji period. These new leaders were faced with the onerous task of replacing the Tokugawan feudal system with more centralized rule and of starting Japan on the road toward technological modernization.

This process required the construction of a centralized administrative structure. The *daimyo* were persuaded to relinquish their land to the emperor's government. They were then assigned prefectures of roughly similar size, to be administered by officials of the central government. *Daimyo* who lost land in the exchange were issued government bonds to make up for the loss. Western-style courts and legal systems were established, as much in an effort to convince Western powers to abandon demands for extraterritoriality (the right of foreigners to be tried by their own judges) as for any other reason. The Japanese developed a modern banking system, and finance, army and navy and education ministries, and they built ports, railways and lighthouses.

To accomplish these changes, the Japanese knew they needed Western technical skills and knowledge. Perry's black ships had made it clear that the Japanese were seriously outgunned by Western military superiority. Many Japanese people, acknowledging the need to catch up with the West technically, felt that their technical primitiveness also indicated cultural backwardness. Western experts were hired to teach in Japan and dozens of young Japanese were sent abroad to study.

Fukuzawa Yukichi emerged as one of the foremost proponents of learning from the West (his face is still on the 10,000-yen note). Fukuzawa travelled to the United States and Europe and wrote a series of books on Western learning and manners. *Seiyō Jiyō* (Conditions in the West), which described everyday social practices and institutions in Western countries, was published in 1866 and quickly became extremely popular. Fukuzawa's books soon made him an acknowledged expert on the West. He was a strong proponent of Western-style democracy and the abolition of the feudal hierarchy. He also believed that people are born equal, and he exhorted them to take control of their own destinies.

The government, in a rare act of self-immolation, undertook to destroy its own class, the samurai. No longer would there be a hereditary élite class; the Meiji oligarchs knew it was time to cast their net more widely for men of talent. Everyone was to be equal and to have equal access to opportunities. Everyone had the right to a family name. The government moved to establish new national standards in 1872. It made four years of education compulsory for every child and established universal conscription the following year. Instead of a large number of samurai armies representing different domains, there would now be one imperial army. No longer were samurai the only people allowed to bear arms. (This development caused a great furor among the peasants as well as the samurai, as universal conscription removed desperately needed help from family farms.) Samurai rice stipends were gradually reduced over a few years and, by 1876, were virtually eliminated. In that same year, the government prohibited the samurai from wearing swords, their badge of honour and prestige. That all of these changes took place in such a short period of time is truly remarkable. In nine years, the samurai were stripped of almost all of their special privileges and status, an act of class aggression all the more remarkable because it was undertaken by samurai leaders.

Not all samurai agreed with these changes. The most powerful challenge to the government's authority was also its final threat—the Satsuma Rebellion of 1877 led by Saigō Takamori, one of the samurai who had toppled the government and installed the emperor in 1868. He left the government in 1873 when his proposal to invade Korea and actively employ the samurai was overruled. He returned home to Satsuma and became the leader of 40,000 samurai who shared his disenchantment. The government decision to abolish the samurai's right to wear swords was the final humiliation. In January of 1877, Saigō led a war against the government. Government forces proved too strong, and by September, the rebellion was quashed.

Saigō committed suicide on the battlefield in quintessential samurai fashion.

By the 1880s, Japanese leaders were becoming increasingly interested in the idea of drafting a constitution. They believed that it would bolster Japanese spirits and loyalty and that it could help convince the Western powers that Japan was a "civilized" country. Ito Hirobumi, a former samurai from Choshu, took charge of the task. He went to Europe to study various European constitutional systems and eventually decided to use the Prussian Constitution as a model. In 1889, the new Constitution came into effect.

The Constitution emphasized the authority of the emperor. He was to exercise all power, oversee all the ministers and hold ultimate command of the army and the navy. In reality, however, the emperor was expected to simply endorse the decisions of his ministers. The emperor appointed the ministers, who were responsible to him rather than to the legislature. The Constitution created a bicameral national assembly. Members of the lower house (House of Representatives) were elected by males paying taxes of fifteen yen or more (about 5 per cent of the male population). The upper house (House of Peers) was composed of appointed members. The lower house alone could pass all permanent laws, while a majority vote in both houses was required for the budget. The Constitution, while not creating a complete democracy, embraced the idea of popular political participation, albeit of a limited sort.

In the 1890s, Japan shifted its attention to international affairs. Its first goal pertaining to foreign policy was to abolish the unequal treaties signed earlier in the century. In 1894, Britain agreed to give up its extraterritorial privileges within five years. Other Western powers soon followed. Although Japan had eliminated the treaties, it continued to try to prove itself the equal of the Western powers. Japan also wanted to ensure its access to the raw materials and markets of Asia and worried that if these Asian countries fell under the control of other powers, Japan would suffer economically.

In 1894, soon after the end of the unequal treaties, Japan declared war on China and began its imperialistic drive, ending its international isolation in dramatic fashion. The Sino-Japanese War was fought over the control of Korea. For security reasons, Japan felt that it could not allow Korea to fall under the control of a third country. Japan easily defeated China, thereby eliminating Chinese influence from the Korean peninsula, and annexed the Chinese island of Taiwan and the southern tip of Manchuria (the Liaotung Peninsula) in the manner of the Western imperialists. Japan was later forced by Russia, with prodding from Germany and France, to give back the Liaotung Peninsula.

The Japanese resented this reversal and sought to ensure that they could not again be ganged up on by the European powers. In 1902, Britain and Japan signed the Anglo-Japanese Alliance, the first agreement between a Western and a non-Western nation that treated both parties as equals. The treaty promised British assistance if Japan were to become involved in a conflict with more than one nation. Through this alliance, Japan earned itself a place on the diplomatic stage. However, the country still worried that the major powers did not take Japan seriously, sensing racial overtones in its interaction with the Western countries.

Japan did not stop with a paper acknowledgement of its new-found status. In 1904, war broke out with Russia, the first major confrontation between a European and an Asian nation. To the surprise of many and the dismay of most Europeans, Japan won handily, gaining mainland territories (which it used as the basis for the subsequent annexation of Korea). Japan had clearly come of age, establishing its military credentials as a major world power and now as a colonizer.

Japan's progress along the path toward Westernization continued apace, faster perhaps than the designers of the Meiji revolution had anticipated. In an illustration of the country's phenomenal capacity for adaptation and imitation, Japan transformed itself within decades into a model Western nation—at least in appearance. The political arena proved particularly fractious as democratic champions struggled against the established authorities, a contest that erupted in the Taisho controversy of 1912–13. This classic conflict in emerging democracies between elected and appointed political officials, was won (at least temporarily) by the elected politicians. Japan's democratization extended to the people in the streets and fields as well, for by 1925 Japan had universal male suffrage.

This stage of the Japanese "miracle"—the rapid Westernization of the former isolationist country—was not without its costs, most of them borne by working people and displaced peasants. Japan's industrialization was a gritty, tough-minded process, marked by appalling working conditions and great hardships for the working poor. On a grander scale, the country's silk trade, which had its own set of abuses, served as the foundation of the export economy. World War I preoccupied European and North American competitors, thus permitting a rapid expansion of the industrial base. But Japan hit the wall at war's end. The return of Western products to the market place damaged the country's newly vibrant industrial economy, and the rapid erosion of the American silk trade (due to the downturn in the American economy and the appearance of synthetic fibres) slowed Japan's economy to a crawl. The resulting turmoil was not evenly shared, falling disproportionately on the tenant farmers and the industrial workers.

The Japan of the 1920s and 1930s bore little resemblance to the country of the late nineteenth century. Democracy ran strong—even rampant—through the countryside. Industrialization had transformed the cities, the work force and the very fabric of society. New ideas, including the radicalization of peasant farmers and workers, flooded into the country, aided by the global preoccupation with the philosophical and political consequences of the Russian Revolution. Business, not so long ago at the bottom of the Japanese social hierarchy, had emerged near the top, increasingly directing the country's leadership and setting the political and diplomatic agenda.

The superficial image of an emerging Westernized country, with all of the excesses and accomplishments of an industrialized nation, masked the deep and immutable "Japaneseness" of Japan. The old leadership had lost both authority and, temporarily, control of the political agenda, but was not gone. More important, the Imperial Army, somewhat brushed aside by the preoccupation with commercial success, longed for the days when Japan's military prowess had vaulted it to international prominence. When the country fell into a deep depression, affecting workers and farmers the most, the vision of a new Japan seemed but a cruel joke. And while many in the country had embraced the new internationalism and welcomed new ideas with enthusiasm, most Japanese longed to return to the era when Japan stood alone, strong and removed from Western influences.

For many Japanese in the 1920s and 1930s, solutions lay in leaving the country. But where to go? Japanese immigrants were unwelcome in many countries, including the major European nations and their former colonial satellites, and the mounting trade restrictions ushered in by the depression slammed one trade door after another. In stepped the Imperial Army. A staged incident in Manchuria in September 1931 provided the pretext for Japanese occupation of the region. Internal political turmoil, capped by a string of assassinations of leading politicians, allowed the army to expand its authority. In a country now rife with instability, the army was one of the few remaining strong and stable elements. Nationwide enthusiasm for the Manchurian action only stiffened the military's resolve and weakened the hand of those who counselled more peaceful approaches. By the end of the 1930s, Japan was again on the rise, but now in a different form. Gone, for a time, was the imitative country of the early twentieth century, eager to catch up with Europe and the United States and to take its place among the industrialized nations. The new Japan was under the control of the military, which was determined to re-instill national pride and to carve out an Asian empire. Patriotism reached a fever pitch, as did political unrest and uncertainty. The world knew, from the Russo-Japanese War of 1904–05, that Japan was capable of great military accomplishments, but it was not prepared for what Japan had in mind.

Canadians in Japan

It is scarcely a surprise that Canada and Japan interacted little before the calamity of World War II. What is surprising is that the countries came together so quickly and strongly after the war. Memories of World War II have generally obscured the pattern of prewar relations, and left the impression that the harmonious, mutually beneficial arrangements of the modern era are a recent development. But Canada and Japan have had strong, if not deep, connections for most of this century, scarred only by the bitter animosities of World War II and the lingering ill will surrounding Canada's anti-Asian sentiments.

One of the many historical oddities of the Canada-Japan relationship is the fact that one of the first English teachers in Japan was a Canadian (born of a Hudson's Bay Company trader father and a West Coast aboriginal mother), Ranald Macdonald. It has been claimed that Macdonald was an American, but although he was born in what is now the United States, then part of the British-controlled Oregon territory, he was a Canadian, and he later lived in Upper Canada. Macdonald signed on to a whaling ship heading to the Far East in 1848, asking in advance to be let off near the island of Hokkaido. He was held under quasi arrest by Japanese authorities in Nagasaki and pressed into service as an English teacher, instructing a handful of Japanese students. One of his students, Enosuke Moriyama, eventually served as an interpreter to Commodore Perry. Macdonald was picked up by another American ship in 1849, and he returned to North America, where he again became active in British Columbia commerce. Given the contemporary prominence of Canadian teachers of English in Japan, and the increasing number of Japanese students studying English in Canada, it is fitting that the first Canadian to reach Japan, years before the county opened to foreigners, would serve as an English instructor.

Canada's first substantial connection to Japan came from another direction—organized religion. So recently a colony, and hence a recipient of the cultural, intellectual and spiritual importations of the empire, Canada quickly transformed its focus to incorporate a fascination with countries and peoples abroad. Canada's Protestant missionary impulse led Canadians to devote more money and contribute more clerics to missionary work in foreign lands than to work among indigenous peoples (and later immigrants) at home; the Roman Catholic Church, although less dramatically, also became interested in missionary work among Asian peoples. While most nationals, therefore, hunkered down to the task of preserving, expanding and solidifying Canada, a small number ventured overseas, determined to spread the word of Christianity among the heathen and pagan nations of the world. Only a handful of others followed in these footsteps, drawn by curiosity or, more commonly, commercial opportunity.

Canadian missionaries moved quickly when the Japanese finally decided in 1873 to open their country to Christianity, lifting an official prohibition on "foreign" religions. Methodist workers Rev. Davidson Macdonald and Rev. George Cochrane were first into the supposedly fertile field, followed by a larger number of Anglicans, Catholics and representatives from other denominations. The more extroverted clerics, such as Methodist Dan Norman, reached thousands of Japanese through their preaching and good works, as the missionaries attempted to demonstrate the suitability of Christian teachings for the Japanese. Church work expanded into various fields, with the establishment of branches of the Young Women's Christian Association in the early twentieth century and, perhaps most significantly, the opening of a sizeable number of Christian and Western-based schools. One of the most influential missionaries was Carolyn MacDonald (1874–1931), a Canadian Presbyterian who spent many years in Japan. She was heavily involved in the establishment of the YWCA, worked closely with women's groups, labour organization, and prison reform. In recognition of MacDonald's work, she was awarded the Sixth Order of Merit of the Order of the Sacred Treasure by the emperor.

In this early period, Canadian authorities also awakened to the commercial possibilities in Japan, appointing a commercial agent in 1897 and sending a display to the Japan Exhibition in Osaka in 1903. In addition, they were quick to realize that Canada's treatment of Japanese immigrants, a subject of great sensitivity in Japan, was a potential source of conflict for future trade possibilities. Trade attracted a handful of Canadians to Japan, establishing the first level of formal relations and providing the first substantial mutually beneficial link between the countries.

All told, Canada had a minimal presence in Japan prior to World War II; in 1938, less than 600 Canadians resided in the country (including a number in Japanese-held territories on the mainland). Missionaries, particularly of the United Church and the Catholic Church, predominated. Their calling was that of Christianity, not Canadianism, and they made few efforts to promote a Canadian outlook (whatever that might have been) among the Japanese. Although many Canadians remained for long periods in Japan, they were sojourners, not migrants, called to Japan to do God's bidding and likely to return to Canada after a suitable period in the field.

The Japanese in Canada

The embargo on emigration from Japan, enforced by the imprisonment of people who returned to the country after being abroad, restricted Japanese migration to Canada until the end of the nineteenth century. The honour of being the "first" Japanese person to live in Canada rests with Manzo "Jack" Nagano, a sailor from Nagasaki, who arrived in British Columbia in 1877. Others followed, but they came in tiny numbers before 1885 and the development of British Columbia that accompanied the completion of the Canadian Pacific Railway. In 1889, the Japanese government established a consulate general's office in Vancouver to handle the increasing interest in migration to British Columbia (a similar office was not set up in Ottawa for another fourteen years). The arrival of Japanese and other Asian peoples, particularly the Chinese, touched off a decades-long spate of xenophobia that dramatically shaped the place of the Japanese in Canadian society and foreshadowed the dramatic and traumatic events of World War II.

That the Japanese migrated at all reflected two developments in Meiji Japan: a relaxation of the prohibition on leaving Japan and a prolonged economic crisis, which encouraged Japanese peasants to seek prosperity outside the country. In the last two decades of the nineteenth century, the exodus began, small in numbers from Japan's perspective, but frightfully large when seen through the race-tinted glasses of North America. Still, by the turn of the century, fewer than 5,000 Japanese had settled in Canada, with the overwhelming majority in British Columbia. Most were recruited by labour contractors to do unskilled work for low wages. The Canadians, lumping the Japanese together with the more numerous Chinese immigrants, lobbied hard for the exclusion of additional Asian migrants. The Japanese government voluntarily limited Japanese migration to Canada, a move that satisfied the government but gave scant reassurance to those hostile to the "Yellow Peril." (The Chinese faced more restrictive measures, including a "head tax," $500 per person, designed to make immigration to Canada prohibitively expensive.)

Anti-Japanese sentiment bubbled to the surface following the Russo-Japanese war, which had confirmed xenophobic concerns about the Japanese "threat." The federal government's belated decision to stand by the Anglo-Japanese treaty of 1894, which assured the Japanese of certain rights within the British Empire, seemed a direct encouragement of Japanese migration. When Japanese immigration to Canada rose dramatically after the war, to roughly 2,000 per year in the first two years, demands for government action escalated, aided by the establishment of the Asiatic Exclusion League and an anti-Japanese riot in Vancouver in 1907. Japanese residents stood up to the rampaging Vancouver crowd and defended their ground, but the escalation in tension was duly noted. The government response was typically Canadian: the establishment of a royal commission led by future prime minister William Lyon Mackenzie King and the dispatching of Rodolphe Lemieux, the minister of labour, to Japan to negotiate with the Japanese. Even at this early juncture, Canadians recognized the significance of Japanese trade with Canada and the direct connection between sensitive immigration matters and future business relations.

The roots of this hostility lay in the fervent Canadian desire to keep the country "white" and to eliminate the unfair competition and social changes associated with Asian immigration. This sentiment was especially strong in British Columbia, where Japanese and Chinese workers had moved quickly into positions on the bottom rungs of the work force and used their savings and initiative to advance into more advantageous positions. The Japanese were particularly active in the fishing industry, soon constituting the largest ethnic group and establishing a notable presence in this important sector. In an age when racist sentiments were widely tolerated, and when politicians successfully campaigned for public office on an anti-Asian platform, the combination of racial attitudes, community fears, and ethnic stereotypes proved to be a potent social and political force.

The Japanese government responded to the Vancouver riot and the Lemieux visit by accepting the so-called Gentlemen's Agreement of 1908. This understanding noted that existing treaties gave Japanese subjects the full and clear right to migrate to Canada, but that Japan would not insist on exercising this right, except for reuniting families and for certain classes of workers. Japanese immigration dropped precipitously, from over 7,500 in 1908 (many stopped in Canada on their way to the United States) to less than a thousand almost every year between 1909 and 1929. Diplomatic accords diffused much of the anti-Asian sentiment, and Japan's dispatch of a naval force to buttress Canada's weak West Coast defences during World War I aided relations considerably. However, Japan's continued aggression in the Far East, particularly the annexation of Korea, touched a deep Canadian nerve, once more fuelling concerns about Japanese designs on the West Coast.

Through this period, the Japanese migrants and their Japanese-Canadian children (nisei) worked to solidify their place within Canadian society. Early migrants had been almost exclusively male; now, larger numbers of women travelled to Canada, often through arranged marriages, to form families and establish deeper roots and communities. The growing solidity of Japanese settlements in Canada only added to white paranoia. The next scare tactic focused on the growth of the Japanese and Japanese-Canadian population—a demographic version of the Asian menace—and the prospect that the fecund Japanese settlers would soon outnumber the non-Asian British Columbians and Canadians.

Although anti-Japanese sentiment abated, exclusionists and anti-Asian groups continuously pushed for restrictions on the newcomers' rights and privileges. They strongly believed that the Japanese were incapable of becoming full members of Canadian society, that they would cling to the strings of the Japanese Empire and that they would never assimilate Canadian values. The anti-Japanese forces were often successful; they limited Japanese rights to secure fishing licences, restricted access to educational opportunities and professional careers, and forced the Japanese into unofficial ethnic enclaves. The Japanese, in the tradition of immigrants attempting to earn their place in a new society, pressed on stoically. Close to 200 volunteered for military service during World War I, presenting Canada with the difficult task of determining if, and where, they could be used. Efforts to gain the rights of citizenship, including equal legal status and the vote, fell far short, overwhelmed by a ground swell of anti-Asian racism.

In the short term, Japanese immigrants and the growing number of Japanese-Canadians could do little to change their lot within Canadian society. Anti-Japanese sentiment rested more on stereotypes than reality, leavened with a healthy dose of Caucasian resentment towards diligent, successful Japanese workers. White British Columbians recoiled at the sight of Japanese fishermen, berry-pickers and store owners, and were suspicious of Japanese intentions regarding the Canadian economy. This fear of Japanese competition complemented the Canadians' preoccupation with Japan's military might, a fear that was realized by Japan's successful campaigns against China and Russia and by the country's growing assertiveness on the world stage.

Faced with occasionally deep resentment, the Japanese and Japanese Canadians persevered. The increasing number of women rounded out Japanese-Canadian society and provided an element of cultural stability. Japanese workers proved themselves, often too well, in various sectors of the British Columbia economy. They dominated the fishing industry until government edicts limited the number of licences they could hold. They moved into forestry until restrictive measures and economic depression forced many out. Many settled into agriculture and commerce, finding new opportunities and few restrictions in these areas. They persisted largely by staying together, tied by the bounds of ancestry, by the work of numerous volunteer associations and churches, and by family and community connections. Like other ethnic minorities in Canada, the Japanese settlers tended to reside together, finding comfort, cultural reinforcement and security in numbers.

Finding succour in predominantly Japanese settlements, and support in Japanese-language institutions and organizations, did little to free the Japanese Canadians from the hostility of their white neighbours. If Japan and Canada proved that two countries could be successful "distant neighbours," the experience of Japanese immigrants and their children in Canada demonstrated that enormous cultural gaps remained between the two peoples. While the Japanese Canadians found tolerance, they also knew the bitter pain of racist criticisms and assaults. Their success and their willful and able adaptation to Canadian customs added to the difficulty, for it reinforced the white Canadians' fear of Asian incursions.

Although East Indians and the Chinese also felt the wrath of Canadian bigotry in the pre–World War II period, the military prowess of the Japanese Imperial Army and the boisterous nationalism of the early twentieth century compounded anti-Japanese feelings. The leap from bigotry and discrimination to hatred and aggressive hostility was a small one, justified by ill-informed opinion and decades of nervousness. Years of coexistence provided an excellent opportunity for Canadians (particularly in British Columbia) to gain a greater understanding of the Japanese and thus form a stronger relationship with their compatriots. But this opportunity was squandered, as racial animosity drove a wedge between the Japanese and the rest of the Canadian population. Having several thousand Japanese and Japanese Canadians in their midst served primarily to harden the opinions of Canadians and to reinforce existing stereotypes and worries.

As tensions mounted in the Pacific over Japan's increasing militarism and expansionism, Canada was far from ready to mediate the growing crisis or to calm the international waters. The Japanese and Japanese Canadians, now numbering over 20,000, felt the acrid breeze of racism. The legacy of diplomacy and cooperation between Canada and Japan, an impressive accomplishment in its own right, stood bashed and bruised by the anti-Japanese sentiment in British Columbia. Few knew precisely what lay ahead, but the rhetoric of the opponents of Asian immigration and memories of riots and discriminatory legislation remained in the minds of many.

Diplomatic Relations

Canada was, until the 1930s, a diplomatic satellite of Great Britain, relying on the mother country for overseas representation and counsel. Slowly, Canada established overseas missions and began to develop the professional foreign service that would be, by the 1950s, among the best in the world. In contrast, Japan moved fairly rapidly in the early twentieth century to create an international presence (largely to encourage overseas trade), to counter the stereotypes about Japanese society, to learn more about industrial advances in the Western world and, increasingly, to defend the interests of Japanese nationals migrating to foreign countries. Not surprisingly, Japan moved first to create a diplomatic presence in Canada, although Canada's moves toward Japan attained prominence in the country's embryonic international operations.

Japan established a consulate general in Vancouver in 1889, in response to the growing number of Japanese immigrants in the province and the mounting criticism towards an Asian presence. In 1903, the Japanese opened an office in Ottawa, a timely step given the growing complexity of Canada-Japan negotiations over immigration. The formal arrangements assisted Canada in responding quickly and efficiently to the furor surrounding the Vancouver Riot of 1907 and facilitated the signing of the Gentlemen's Agreement of 1908 in which Japan voluntarily slowed migration to Canada. The existence of treaties between Britain and Japan (accords to which Canada was, as a member of the British Empire, automatically tied) set the parameters for Canadian action. The Anglo-Japanese Alliance, signed in 1902, made Japan an ally of Canada, at least through the troubled years of World War I. When the accord came up for renewal again in 1921, Prime Minister Arthur Meighen played an important role in having the agreement scrapped in favour of the Four Power Treaty (between Britain, Japan, the United States and France). Canada signed as a member of the British delegation.

Canada moved more slowly in international affairs. The government appointed its first trade representative in 1897, and, continuing its efforts to stimulate trade with Japan, opened a trade office in Yokohama in 1904 (which was moved to Tokyo in 1923). Relying on British diplomats to handle Canadian consular matters proved adequate for years, but Canada gradually accepted the need for a more direct presence in Japan. In 1928, the federal government negotiated the exchange of ministers between Canada and Japan and announced that Herbert Marler, a former Liberal cabinet minister, would be Canada's first minister to Japan. One year later, Marler assumed control of the Canadian legation, which included among its small staff, Hugh Keenleyside as first secretary and chargé d'affaires (who would become one of Canada's most prominent and important mandarins). It was highly significant that the establishment of the Japan mission came quickly on the heels of Canada's tentative first steps into the diplomatic arena—to Washington and Paris, to supplement a long-standing presence in London.

Japan moved at the same time to add to its consular presence and to establish a formal diplomatic structure in Canada. Prince Iyemasa Tokugawa, the first Japanese minister to Canada, arrived in Ottawa in the fall of 1929. Tokugawa, who remained for five years, found himself a busy man, particularly as military conflicts expanded through the early 1930s. The two countries were at odds over the

Japanese invasion of Manchuria, when Japan faced censure at the League of Nations and walked out of the assembly. Although Canada had supported the league's position against Japan, diplomatic relations remained on an even keel, primarily because of the growing importance of Canada's trade with Japan and limited Canadian interest in the geopolitics of the Far East. Trade talks, particularly concerning restrictive tariffs, kept the diplomats busy, but they could not prevent a precipitous decline in Canadian exports to Japan through the 1930s.

Even Japan's increased aggression after 1937 did not change Canada's approach to Japan, although tensions continued to escalate (for example, Rev. Marcel Fournier, a Dominican Father, was charged with spying on behalf of Canada). Canadians in Asia occasionally found themselves trapped in the path of Japanese armies or attacked by antiforeigner mobs in Japan; there were a number of deaths and considerable property damage, not the least of which was an attack on the *Empress of Asia*, operated by Canadian Pacific. Anti-Asian sentiment continued to grow in British Columbia, leading to renewed demands for restrictions on Japanese immigration. The breach deepened when Japan announced its decision to join Germany and Italy, and form the Axis alliance. Demands for the cessation of Canadian trade with the increasingly bellicose Japanese escalated. Although Japan did not join Germany and Italy in the European War, which started in 1939, future battle lines had been clearly drawn: Canada would stand by its historic partners, Britain and France, and Japan would follow its new allies, Germany and Italy.

***

Much had changed in less than seventy years. Both Canada and Japan had undergone dramatic transformations and come of age internationally—Japan as a major military force and Canada, as a middle power. From the beginning, the relationship was characterized by official politeness and grass-roots uneasiness, particularly on the Canadian side of the Pacific. Japan, indeed the entire Orient, was more than mysterious and exotic; it was, to many Canadians, dangerous, militaristic and unpredictable. Christian churches and government officials had made efforts to bridge the cultural and geographic gap, but these efforts resulted in limited success. Trade ties illustrated that mutual interest could overcome formidable barriers of attitude and stereotype, but outbreaks of violence in both countries, and hostility to foreigners remained the hallmarks of the Canada-Japan relationship. Now a greater test—a global conflagration—confronted both nations.

3

War without Mercy: Canada and Japan during World War II

The Pacific War ended on August 9, 1945—or at least the fighting stopped. The laying down of arms, followed by the Allied occupation, Japanese supplication, and the rapid reinstatement of Japan as a favoured trading partner gave every external indication of countries able to put the war far behind them.

Yet the legacy of World War II lives on strongly in the minds of Canadians and the Japanese. There is more to the folk memory of the war than the monuments in Hiroshima and Nagasaki, which memorialize the tens of thousands killed by the atomic bombs; more than lingering Canadian animosity about the treatment of Canadian soldiers and prisoners of war during and after the fall of Hong Kong in December 1941. Often unstated, often unconscious, is the recollection that Canada and Japan were mortal enemies, sworn to kill soldiers, undermine civilian morale and bring the other to its knees.

Movies and popular culture have trivialized World War II, turning it into a military struggle between competing armies, and obscuring the intensity of the conflict on both sides of the Pacific. The friendliness of the postwar relationship, which gives cause to hide the bad blood of earlier years, has the same effect. But the memory is there—potent and important. Canadians lived in fear of being overrun by the Yellow Peril, armed to the teeth with guns, bombers, battleships and a suicidal commitment to the emperor and the country. Canadians gave their all for the war effort, throwing their support behind rationing campaigns, victory bond drives and military recruitment campaigns. The Japanese, stirred to war by patriotic appeals to help the country reach its national destiny, approached World War II with steely determination. This was Japan's war to the end, epitomized by acts of military suicide, by kamikaze pilots and youngsters in Okinawa who ran into the invader's military emplacements carrying armed explosives on their backs.

In the 1930s, Japanese expansionism strained relations, for Canada supported efforts by the League of Nations to curb international aggression and attempted, with no great success, to limit Japanese activities. By then, Canadian trade with Japan had reached sizeable proportions, and economic considerations, together with a desire to maintain positive relations with Japan, limited Canadian criticisms. Canada established a trade surplus with Japan in 1922, and by 1929, the country shipped over $42 million in exports to Japan while importing less than $13 million in Japanese goods. Trade peaked at that point and declined steadily through the 1930s, to only $10.3 million in Canadian exports and $3.8 million in imports from Japan in 1933. This decline reflected the political difficulties associated with Japan's increasing aggressiveness in the Far East. The value of Japanese imports dropped steadily through the 1930s, and importing slowed dramatically when the federal government slapped a tariff worth one-third of the goods' value on Japanese products.

In the later part of the decade, Canadian groups began to organize boycotts of Japanese goods. The boycott campaigns capitalized on two well-springs of anti-Japanese feeling in Canada: opposition to Japanese aggression in China, and the long-standing animosity to Japanese immigration to Canada. Immigration from Japan had dropped steeply, to slightly over 100 people per year in the 1930s, but such hard evidence did little to deter the anti-Asian advocates who wanted to at least prohibit Japanese immigration, if they could not deport people of Japanese ancestry. Japan's bellicosity only added fuel to the smouldering flames of racism and exclusionism, and to the increasing fear of Japanese militarism.

Japanese Aggression

Despite minor diplomatic efforts and the uniting effects of international trade, Canadians left no doubts as to their primary allegiance. in the late 1930s, when Japan joined the Germany-Italy Axis, Canada stood staunchly behind Britain. In fact, Canada was counting on American military might to defend it against possible Japanese attack; given Canada's size and nature, there was little possibility that the small Canadian army would be able to mount much of a defence against the formidable Japanese naval and air forces.

As tensions increased, particularly after the outbreak of war in Europe, Canada kept an increasingly nervous eye on Japan. The government even established a Special Committee on Asians in British Columbia in October 1940; this group called for the voluntary registration of all persons of the "Japanese race," an exercise carried out by the RCMP in 1941. That summer, prodded by British and American action, the Canadian government froze Japanese assets in Canada and halted the shipment of strategic minerals to Japan. This suspension was quickly expanded to include nonmilitary items, such as wheat and timber. Japanese representatives in Ottawa protested the decisions, but failed to overturn them.

Simmering anti-Japanese sentiment in Canada threatened to boil over at any moment. Few Canadians differentiated between the Japanese and the thousands of Japanese-Canadians in the country. Japanese Canadians did not enjoy full citizenship rights, could not vote in elections or hold certain professional licences, and were not welcomed into the Canadian armed forces. Now, as storm clouds stirred over the Pacific, Japanese Canadians carried the added, and inappropriate, burden of being perceived as the potential "enemy within," a formidable "fifth column" (a base for attacking forces), strategically placed on the nation's vulnerable West Coast.

The Japanese, their aggressiveness fuelled by successive victories against China and the growing imperialism of a nation in arms, were equally concerned about the Canadians in their midst. In the 1930s, a few hundred Canadians lived in Japan: missionaries, a few business people and a handful of government officials. But as Japan's successes mounted, so did Japanese distaste for *gaijin* (foreigners). Japanese outrage surfaced in bomb attacks on Canadian missions, the murder of several priests, and other assaults on Canadian property and personnel. In the time-honoured tradition of countries preparing for war, both Canadian and Japanese hatred and fear of the "other" escalated.

World War II began with several regional pressure points, gradually expanding into a global conflict. Long before Pearl Harbor, the official start of the Pacific War in the minds of most North Americans, the Japanese had commenced their expansion and launched a major military campaign against Pacific rivals. Through the 1910s and 1920s, Japan had solidified its status as a major military power, through the defeat of Russia and successful contests with China. The isolationism of the previous century long since dispatched, Japan sought international prestige and standing. More than that, the country desired new lands, additional resources and the economic clout that accompanied a well-controlled empire. Having proved its mettle against Russia early in the century, Japan now flexed its muscles against Asian countries.

Japan's expansion began in 1931 with the occupation of Manchuria. The establishment of a puppet government in Manchuko (Manchuria) gave Japan effective control over sizeable mainland holdings and foreshadowed the more aggressive campaign against China. The conflict broke out in 1937, when a manufactured "incident" was used to justify a Japanese attack. Japan moved quickly and destructively through northern China, taking major cities—Peking (Beijing), Tianjin, Shanghai and Nanking—and laying waste to much of the countryside. In all respects, it was an awesome military display, played out far from European and North American eyes and attracting relatively little attention outside of Asia.

The Imperial Army, however, had no intention of stopping. To the south lay greater rewards: Hong Kong, Singapore, the Philippines and Indonesia. For the more aggressive military leaders, other targets loomed: Alaska and North America's West Coast, Hawaii and Australia. Pumped by victory, fuelled by enthusiasm for the emperor and increasingly convinced of its invincibility, the Japanese army tolerated few constraints. By late 1939, Japanese forces started to circle China from the south, cutting off valuable supply lines to Indonesia. The advances came at considerable cost, both in human and financial terms, and dissension about the lingering Chinese conflict grew on the home front. But Japan pressed on, determined to hold China against Chiang Kai Shek's armies and to use the mainland as a base for future attacks against Hong Kong, Singapore and points further south. In that direction lay the oil-rich lands of the Dutch East Indies, which constituted Japan's chance to escape from an American-imposed oil embargo and to secure an independent supply of this vital resource.

As the imperial forces prepared for the push south, another threat loomed: the United States, protector of the Philippines and, despite decades of isolationism, a potent threat in the Pacific. While it was possible, in the Eurocentric times of the 1930s and 1940s, to remain little more than a spectator to Japanese aggression against Asian states (a series of military atrocities that would have generated a strong reaction had they been targeted at European foes), the United States could not ignore the December 7, 1941, assault on its Pacific fleet and air installations in Hawaii. The Japanese attack on Pearl Harbor, the subject of intense debate among the imperial forces for years, raised the war to new heights. Japan and its Asian puppet states were poised, with their millions of people and fanatical armies, to move against North America. The mythical Yellow Peril of the nineteenth century had now taken military form.

Japan quickly reached its peak. Although the attack on Pearl Harbor proved not to be a crucial blow, it left the Pacific fleet crippled. Coinciding with the attack on Hawaii, Japanese forces moved into the Philippines, Indochina, Thailand, Malaya and Hong Kong. With a speed that rivalled the Nazi blitzkrieg, and with a ferocity and tenacity unmatched in the war, the imperial forces pushed back defenders to lay claim to vast territories. The process stretched the Japanese Empire to its limit; by early 1942, the Japanese forces were widely dispersed, in the Aleutian Islands, China and the Philippines, and on dozens of small islands in the Pacific. North America and Australia appeared, logically, to be the next targets. The Japanese onslaught turned the war into a truly global conflict, leaving few corners of the world untouched.

Canada's Role in World War II

If Japan was, before the war, a minor player on the world scene, Canada was inconsequential. With only a handful of consulates in the capitals of major trading partners, including Japan, and still perceived as a diplomatic "child" of Britain, the country had minimal status in international affairs. The Canadian government, led by continentalist Prime Minister King, sought to loosen ties with England, strengthen political connections to the United States and establish a greater measure of international credibility. But through the economic wreckage of the Great Depression, Canadians were preoccupied with internal and economic crises, and remained mute observers of the international scene.

Generations-old connections to Great Britain and other European nations ensured, however, that the turmoil looming over Europe did not pass unnoticed. By the late 1930s, after appeasement had failed to stifle German ambitions, and with the inherent wickedness of the Nazi government revealed through escalating state-sponsored violence and public attacks on Jews and intellectuals, a military crisis appeared unavoidable. Britain and France opted to draw the line with Poland, counting on their now steely determination to stare down German expansionism.

The gamble, one of many in the years leading up to World War II, failed miserably. Unplacated after nonmilitary take-overs of Austria and Czechoslovakia, the Germans turned their military machinery loose on Poland. Britain and France responded with uncharacteristic resolve, declaring war against Germany on September 3, 1939. Canadians watched the escalating conflict with eagerness and dismay, for many shared European concerns about Nazi aggression, while others, particularly in Quebec, wondered about the appropriateness of Canada's once again joining a European conflict. Unlike the situation during World War I, however, Canada was not automatically at war just because Britain had taken the plunge. It took an act of the Canadian Parliament to bring Canada into the war. Prime Minister King waited one week—long enough to make a clear statement of Canadian independence, but not long enough to anger those demanding that Canada prove its support of Britain—before asking Parliament for a declaration of war.

Canada's attentions would, for most of the war, be directed toward Europe. The country made an impressive industrial contribution to Britain's supplies and sent hundreds of thousands of troops to England to assist with the island's defence and, once the threat of attack had passed, to prepare for the liberation of Europe. Through the British Commonwealth Air Training Plan, Canada aided in the preparation of thousands of pilots and flight crew members from throughout the Commonwealth, many of whom served with distinction in the vital Battle of Britain. Until VE Day, May 8, 1945, and the surrender of Nazi Germany, Canadians were preoccupied with European battles and preparations; the battle for the Pacific was left in the hands of the Americans.

Canadians did not completely ignore Japan and the Japanese threat in the months after September 1939. The rhetoric and fearmongering about the Yellow Peril resonated in parts of the country, particularly in British Columbia. Some rabid opponents of Asian immigration proposed preemptive action against residents of Japanese ancestry, to ensure that there were no fifth column activities similar to those experienced in the Philippines and elsewhere. Faced with the daunting task of defending the intricate and harsh West Coast, the Canadian government took only meagre measures: gun emplacements on Point Grey in Vancouver and near Victoria, several small military establishments on the west coast of Vancouver Island and near Prince Rupert. Until the attack on Pearl Harbor in December 1941, however, Japan remained a rather distant threat, certainly far less ominous and immediate than Nazi Germany. With the Japanese attack on the United States, and simultaneous assaults on British-held territory, Canada wasted no time in joining the fray. On December 7, 1941, without recalling Parliament as he had done to declare war on Germany, Prime Minister King informed the Japanese government that Canada was officially at war with Japan—beating both the British and the Americans to the punch.

Canada's involvement in the Pacific theatre predated the outbreak of war. Prodded by Britain to participate in the defence of the British Empire's Pacific colonies, Canada agreed to send a small number of soldiers to Hong Kong. The Canadian government approached the matter with less than burning urgency; a Japanese attack on the British colony appeared unlikely, and Canadian troops had not been trained for the unusual conditions of Asian service. The Canadian army dispatched two battalions, the Winnipeg Grenadiers and the Royal Rifles of Canada, to Hong Kong in November 1941. Close to two thousand men found themselves heading across the Pacific Ocean to take up stations against the encroaching Japanese army. Then, and later, Canadians wondered about the logic of dispatching soldiers to the highly vulnerable British colony.

Japanese forces attacked the Allied troops in Hong Kong in December 1941. What followed was one of the most bitter and costly reversals in Canadian military history. The Japanese attacked relentlessly. The still-raw Canadian troops were pressed immediately into a vicious battle, struggling desperately to hold on to small bits of territory. While the Commonwealth troops requited themselves with honour and courage, they could not withstand the withering assaults by the much larger, more powerful enemy. On Christmas Day, Hong Kong fell, touching off a murderous spree by the victors, who ran amuck among prisoners, injured soldiers and medical staff, killing dozens. Roughly 300 Canadian soldiers were killed; almost 1,700 taken prisoner.

The nightmare continued after the battle. Canadian soldiers discovered that the international conventions of war were not observed by the Japanese. Many suffered brutally at the hands of their captors, as did thousands of Hong Kong civilians who, like the Chinese before them, learned how uncontrolled the Japanese forces were when flushed with the adrenalin surge of military conquest. Canadian survivors were packed off to Japanese war camps, living hells that left the soldiers emaciated and ill. Those with the strength were forced to work, in keeping with international convention, but conditions fell far short of established standards. Having surrendered in the first weeks of Canadian combat with Japan, the Hong Kong survivors remained in Japanese hands until the final months of the war. The much smaller number of soldiers still alive at war's end bore deeper physical and psychological scars from the experience; their anger would linger long after Japan's surrender.

Japan's military might seemed unstoppable. Pearl Harbor lay in smouldering ruins (although the damage proved less serious than initially thought), Hong Kong (followed shortly by Singapore and the Philippines) was in Japanese hands, and the Imperial Army appeared determined to continue its expansion. Australia braced itself for a possible invasion, and far to the North, the prospect of a Japanese assault on North America seemed possible, if not imminent. The Japanese invasion of the Aleutian islands of Kiska and Attu provided further proof of Japan's insatiable appetite for conquest.

Japanese forces moved into the Aleutian Islands in June 1942, encountering no resistance in these far-flung American islands. American and Canadian forces moved to halt the Japanese advance, seemingly intended as a diversionary tactic, and launched a series of air attacks on Japanese positions. In the spring and summer of 1943, the combined forces reclaimed the Aleutian Islands from determined Japanese troops. The Aleutian campaign may have been minor in broader strategic terms—the Japanese had some 2,500 men on Attu and another 5,400 on Kiska—but it helped entrench North American fears of the Japanese menace. The Japanese army suffered grievously at Attu—over 2,300 Japanese soldiers died in the battle for Attu alone and less than a dozen Japanese soldiers survived—and hundreds died by their own hand, many in suicide charges at American positions. The battle confirmed the North American belief that the Japanese placed a different value on life. Japan would be a formidable and intractable foe.

Canada had responded to the Japanese advance by strengthening its military presence along the West Coast, although the country had precious few resources to spread across its vast expanses. Two divisions were mobilized for the defence of the West Coast with over 35,000 soldiers. Several groups of conscripts, derisively called "Zombies" by those who thought that all young men should want to join the army, were sent west to prepare for the defence of the continent. Canada committed sizeable forces to the recapture of the Aleutian Islands, including four air squadrons in Alaska and 4,800 Canadian troops mobilized for the final assault on Kiska (part of a 34,000-troop Allied force). These troops did not face combat at Kiska, as the Japanese evacuated their remaining soldiers in a daring, fog-shrouded naval manoeuvre.

The United States was more concerned than the Canadian government about possible Japanese attacks. Within weeks of the Pearl Harbor debacle, American authorities approached Canada to discuss the need for expanded military facilities in the far northwest. The United States was anxious to build a highway to Alaska, expand a series of airfields between Edmonton, Alberta, and Fairbanks, Alaska, and construct various related projects, including a pipeline-refinery complex to supply military units to the northwest. The Canadian government did not share the Americans' sense of urgency and declined the opportunity to participate in the projects; however, Canada would not stand in the way of America's desire to proceed.

The Northwest Defence Projects redesigned northwestern Canada, and the heavy publicity given to the initiatives sent the comforting message that the Americans were sparing no expense in preparing for continental defence. But by the time the highway project was half-completed, Japanese military reversals in the Aleutians and, particularly, in the Midway islands in June 1942, turned the tide of the war. The Japanese advance had been checked, and Allied forces, led by the Americans, were now pressing the Imperial Army and Navy back toward Japan. The downgrading of military construction projects in the far northwest would ultimately limit their utility as part of the region's economic development. But with the war still raging, few could protest the American decision to assign a much lower priority to the highway and related initiatives.

Canadians participated minimally in the rest of the Pacific War. Royal Canadian Air Force personnel flew supply missions in Burma and Ceylon (Sri Lanka), where Squadron Leader L.J. Birchall played a primary role in alerting the Allies to an imminent Japanese assault on the island. The Royal Canadian Navy vessel *Uganda* served briefly in the Pacific in 1945, participating in the Allied attack on the Caroline Islands.

Treatment of Japanese Canadians

For Canadians, the war in the Pacific was unusual, for the enemy lurked threateningly over the horizon—unseen, unknown, but feared nonetheless. A half-century's worth of anti-Japanese rhetoric, and the rapid dispatch of Allied forces at Hong Kong and elsewhere, fuelled the imagination and sparked endless fears about Japanese attacks on the West Coast. The knowledge that Japanese residents in other countries, principally the Philippines, had served as a fifth column heightened suspicions about the more than 20,000 people of Japanese ancestry living in British Columbia.

The ever anxious Prime Minister King twitched nervously about the prospects in British Columbia. Racists seized the opportunity to promote long-standing hatred; those fearful of a Japanese attack worried about the military threat to British Columbia. Others were concerned that the growing anti-Japanese sentiment would result in a racist backlash against the peaceful Japanese Canadians. Together, and with few dissenting voices save for the Japanese Canadians themselves, they demanded action from Ottawa.

And Ottawa responded. Most Japanese language newspapers were closed, Japanese nationals were forced to register with the government, and a mass effort commenced to strip people of Japanese ancestry of their cars, boats, homes and businesses, and of their right to live near the coast. The "evacuation" of the Japanese Canadians, which followed on the heels of an American decision to relocate people of Japanese ancestry from coastal areas, was conducted in polite Canadian fashion between February and October 1942; under the all-encompassing power of the War Measures Act and the supervision of a special government agency set up for the task, the government ordered the removal of people of Japanese ancestry from the area. The story is familiar to some Canadians: the initial displacement to the exhibition grounds in Vancouver, where families were separated and forced to live in converted showrooms and stock pens, the use of young, able-bodied men in road and construction camps, the relocation of many to abandoned mining towns in the British Columbia interior, and the subsequent removal of many to "safer" locations in Alberta, Manitoba or Ontario. Other elements of the evacuation included curfews, confiscation and resale (at rock-bottom prices) of personal effects, and the loss of title to fishing boats and farms.

The government's quick action—shown by hindsight to be unnecessary, given the lack of evidence of Japanese or Japanese-Canadian efforts to assist an invasion—placated a West Coast population driven to near panic by the prospect of having thousands of "enemies" living among them. For this action, Prime Minister King claimed something of a victory, since there were few outbreaks of racially motivated violence and no large-scale riots or demonstrations. The action, of course, simply transferred the pain and suffering to the Japanese and Japanese Canadians, who endured the indignity of being shuffled into stockyards, separated from family members, stripped of personal belongings and hard-won private wealth, and relegated to distant camp sites for the duration of the war.

A lesser-known aspect of the evacuation process was the internment of people of Japanese ancestry in Canadian prisoner-of-war camps. Immediately after the commencement of war with Japan, several dozen Japanese suspected of "subversive intentions" were arrested. Those deemed to be serious cases, male Japanese nationals and anyone who protested the internments, were sent to camps in Angler and Petawawa, Ontario, where they spent most of the war behind barbed wire. By the summer of 1942, over 650 people of Japanese descent were in the Angler, Ontario, prisoner-of-war camp. The internees were a varied lot, ranging from those who protested their abiding loyalty to Canada to others who wore their Japanese loyalties on their sleeves. None had committed a crime save that of being of Japanese ancestry and protesting the internment. Inmates suffered the inevitable loss of freedom, emotional damage and the indignity of living under constant supervision, although they received adequate food, medical care and clothing.

Canadian Prisoners of War

On the other side of the Pacific, the experience of Canadian prisoners of war followed a very different path. From the outbreak of war, Canada and Japan were very much aware that a number of their nationals remained in enemy hands. The fall of Hong Kong, alone, put several thousand Canadians into Japanese prisoner-of-war camps. The Canadian government remained acutely aware that the treatment of Japanese nationals and people of Japanese ancestry in Canada would be closely watched by the Japanese government and might well influence Japanese treatment of Canadians in custody. As the authors of *Mutual Hostages*, a study of Japanese-Canadian relations during World War II, concluded: "The Japanese Canadians, including those who were Canadian nationals by birth or naturalization, effectively became hostages for Canadians in Japanese hands" (p. 101).

The internment of Canadians in Japan did not match the evacuation and internment of people of Japanese ancestry in Canada. In Japan, a handful of civilians, most of them missionaries, were placed under supervision or in camps for the duration of the war: this process accelerated when Canadian and American authorities rounded up Japanese people in North America. Conditions and treatment of internees in Japan varied widely. Food supplies were rarely adequate, and Japanese officers often treated the Canadians with disdain. In a few exceptional cases, missionaries were tortured and murdered by guards, and several camps, such as the notorious Stanley Camp in Hong Kong, held inmates in inexorable conditions. A substantial number of the civilian internees were repatriated during the war, as part of an exchange with Japan. The remaining Canadian civilians lived through many of the hardships of the native residents, for the war years saw a massive diversion of food and material to military purposes and required major sacrifices; otherwise, these Candians encountered relatively few difficulties.

Military prisoners of war fared much worse. International conventions permitted the use of captured soldiers as workers, and labour shortages in Japan ensured that this option was exercised. Almost 1,200 of the men captured in Hong Kong were shipped to Japan in 1943 and 1944 to work, mostly in the mines. Brutal conditions, cruel guards, inadequate food and limited health care combined to make the prisoner's lot a miserable one. Over one-quarter of all Canadian soldiers taken into custody in Hong Kong died in Japanese prisoner-of-war camps, a total of 136 deaths in Japan and 128 in Hong Kong. (For comparison, the death rate in German prisoner-of-war camps was 4 per cent.) Vicious beatings, inadequate food and miserable living conditions all claimed their victims. Freedom only alleviated the prisoners' suffering, for they carried home the psychological scars of their mistreatment, injuries and diseases.

Although Germany finally laid down its arms and surrendered on May 7, 1945, war continued in the Pacific. Canadians wished to celebrate, and to put the depredations and sacrifices of war far behind them. But there were battles still to be fought and won, alongside the American armies then island-hopping their way toward Japan. Japan, ferocious and unrelenting in victory, looked to be as single-minded and unforgiving in defeat. The Allied powers, principally the United States, totalled up the likely costs of a direct invasion of Japan, and recoiled at the prospect. In 1943 and 1944, only a handful of Canadian military personnel remained in the Pacific; as the final battle against Japan neared, it became evident that the country needed more than a token force.

The Defeat of Japan

The Canadian authorities decided to make a significant military contribution to the American assault on Japan. In April 1945, the country established the Canadian Army Pacific Command, and re-

ceived almost 80,000 volunteers, of whom less than half were deemed suitable for combat. (All Canadian military personnel were
asked if they wished to join the Pacific force. The men aboard the
Canadian ship *Uganda*, which had previously served in the Pacific,
voted not to return to the Pacific theatre.) Before Canadian troops
could take their place among the Allied fighting forces, the war took
a dramatic turn. Today, historians still debate the logic behind the
American decision to drop one atomic bomb on Hiroshima on August
6, 1945, followed by a second on Nagasaki three days later. In a
matter of seconds, nuclear explosions and the resulting fire-storms
demolished entire cities, laying waste to buildings and killing tens of
thousands of people, mostly civilians. The dropping of the atomic
bombs would stand as both the final, decisive act of World War II
and the initial spark of the postwar nuclear terror. Whatever the
reasons for testing this most awesome of weapons, the wholesale
destruction of two Japanese cities had the desired effect.

On August 14, 1945, Japan surrendered to General Douglas Mac-
Arthur, Supreme Commander for the Allied Powers for the Occupation and Control of Japan. The following day, Emperor Hirohito went
on radio to explain to the Japanese people that, despite their valiant
efforts, surrender was unavoidable in order to prevent complete destruction of Japan itself. (The Japanese public had never before heard
the emperor's voice, and he spoke in an imperial dialect that was
unknown to most Japanese. Japanese citizens recoiled at the sound,
and shock, of hearing the emperor speak, almost as much as at the
message itself.)

Japan's approach to the war, described by foreigners as fanatical,
had consumed the Japanese for more than eight years. At the height
of its military success, Japan commanded territory stretching from
Alaska to Indonesia, and was regarded as one of the most powerful
countries in the world. In 1945, only three years later, Japan's dreams
of an empire were shattered, and the country was forced into a
national process of supplication at the feet of the more powerful
Americans. The Japanese faced the unthinkable. Emperor Hirohito,
viewed by his subjects as almost godlike, had asked the people to
accept surrender; the resounding assurances of imminent victory and
permanent glory that had justified the sacrifices and monumental war
effort now rang hollow. Defeat in war is humiliating and demoralizing. To the Japanese in 1945, it came on the heels of two years of
military reversals, abundant evidence of the strain of warfare, and
the stark, painful reality of the fire-bombed remnants of Tokyo and

the ashes of Hiroshima and Nagasaki; defeat meant the end of the world as they knew it. For the first time in the nation's history, a conquering nation would occupy its shores, direct its governments, control its economy, and dictate to its people.

In contrast, for most Canadians, war in the Pacific was always more a possibility than a fact. Before the Japanese attack on Pearl Harbor, West Coast Canadians worried about a Japanese invasion and about the possible threat from within. The attack never came, save for the comparatively small assault on the American Aleutian Islands, and Canadians and Canadian soil emerged from the war unscathed. The tragedy in Hong Kong claimed over 900 dead and wounded, and the total Canadian losses for the Pacific War amounted to "only" 730 dead and 430 wounded—a far cry from the devastating losses associated with Canadian involvement in the war in Europe. (In total, around 45,000 Canadian military personnel were killed or deemed missing, out of a total military complement of 780,000. Japan's losses, in contrast, equalled a staggering 1.3 million military deaths and over 1 million civilian fatalities.)

But the absence of prolonged Canadian combat with Japan or of a Japanese attack on Canada did not make the conflict any less real. Japan posed a grave threat, as its major victories in 1941 and 1942 revealed with distressing clarity. The war proved one thing: that it was very wrong to underestimate the Japanese or to assume that their actions and motivations could be readily understood in Canadian terms. Canadians found few opportunities for retribution; the war ended before Canadian troops were involved in a major way, but the Canadian War Crimes Liaison Detachment in Japan ensured that prison camp guards accused of mistreating Canadian soldiers were brought forward for trial. All but one of those accused were found guilty.

Japan now faced a daunting prospect: rebuilding from the suffering and sacrifices of a war that had sapped the country of its wealth and industrial vitality and that had saddled the nation with the image of an international pariah. Images of the evil-grinning "Nip," the kamikaze fighter pilot, the "inscrutable" Japanese, would become deeply fixed in the North American imagination through the efforts of wartime propagandists and postwar movie producers. While Japan tried, and largely succeeded, in passing off its own version of the origins, nature and atrocities of the war for domestic consumption, North Americans did their best to draw attention to Japanese aggressiveness, viciousness and inhumanity. From the ravages of war emerge great powers or humbled nations; with the American-led occupation forces enveloping the Japanese countryside, it was not at all clear which option awaited the once-powerful country.

Canada faced a different fear: returning to a prewar depression that had drained the economic and social vitality from the country. During the war years, when the ideas of deficit financing and government intervention enjoyed greater public acceptance, the government introduced the first elements of the new Canadian welfare state. At war's end, a continued commitment to social and economic reform created bold new visions of a country without unemployment, with national housing schemes and expanded educational opportunities. And so Canada sought to build off its successes—the mobilization of tens of thousands of military personnel, the development of a national will to combat a shared enemy, and the significant expansion of industrial capacity—to create postwar stability and growth. At the end of World War I, the release of thousands of soldiers into the workforce and the collapse of government spending had generated economic and labour problems across the country. In 1945 the Canadian government sought to prevent these postwar problems and prove to Canadians that the sacrifices and contributions of the war years would be rewarded with prosperity and peace.

The end of the war did not, in any practical sense, end hostilities between Canada and Japan, even though the nation of the rising sun had been battered to its knees. As the prisoners of war returned, and recounted their horror stories from the internment camps, Canadians renewed their anguish and their animosity toward the Japanese. Seven years passed before Canada and Japan reestablished full diplomatic relations. Propagandists in Canada, the United States and Japan worked hard to stir up racial animosity toward the enemy, and largely succeeded. Although the tap of government-sponsored hate imagery was turned off, memories remained, as did the deeply ingrained frustrations of years lost, and the personal suffering.

Canadians also continued to wrestle with the postwar fallout from the internment of Japanese Canadians. At the end of the war, the federal government encouraged people of Japanese ancestry to return to Japan; a substantial number, angered by their treatment during the internment, complied (although many subsequently returned to Canada). Those remaining in Canada were not allowed to return to the British Columbian coast, a sign that the wartime hostilities had not yet evaporated. Having paid a high price for their heritage and having accepted the relocation and losses with amazing stoicism, the Japanese Canadians began their quest for compensation and recognition. The government's meagre response came grudgingly: Those who lost property received partial repayment, but only if they signed a form waiving all future claims against the Canadian government. And Japanese-Canadian citizens gained the right to vote in 1947, a fundamental benefit of citizenship. Almost forty years later, the Canadian government tendered a formal apology and provided compensation to victims of the wartime incarceration.

***

World War II in the Pacific was, as historian John Dower described it, a "war without mercy." Japan and the Allied powers entered the conflict with an unwavering determination that was sustained by growing racial hatred on both sides of the ocean. When the United States dropped the atomic bomb, punctuating its declaration of military prowess, Japan had no choice but to surrender, an act of national humiliation that would not soon be forgotten.

A different world emerged from the ashes of war. America had shed its isolationism, and expanded its military presence throughout the region; commerce and American imperialism followed in the army's path. Japan had lost all of its gains, and stood humbled and demoralized, visions of national greatness relegated to the historians and dreamers. The current struggle was to survive and rebuild, neither of which was assured in the economic and social devastation of postwar Japan. Canada's role was peripheral in the postwar Pacific. Canadians no longer faced the threat of Japanese invasion, but the realization of their own racist actions during the war had sullied the nation's military accomplishments. The country was economically strong, although burdened with a massive debt. and uncharacteristically confident, as the result of an enormous national war effort.

The Pacific world would, in the aftermath of Pearl Harbor, Midway and Hiroshima, have to be remade. In the fall of 1945, few would have anticipated Japan's remarkable recovery. There is an old saying: To the victor go the spoils. Not in the case of World War II.

4

Canada-Japan Relations after World War II

The cessation of armed combat in 1945 did not end the war, any more than the signing of the armistice in November 1918 stalled the effects of World War I. America saw the opportunity to exact a further price, and to impose its will on the vanquished. Japan was truly defeated by the end of the fighting. Its major cities lay in ruins: Tokyo had been massively damaged by conventional bombing, Hiroshima and Nagasaki had been devastated by atomic bombs and Okinawa had been laid to waste by the American invasion. Only the ancient city of Kyoto had escaped destruction at the hands of the Allied forces. The Japanese people were exhausted, the economy lay in tatters, starvation was rampant and the prospects for a return to the prosperity that had fuelled the empire looked dim indeed.

And Emperor Hirohito had signed the act of surrender, a painful acknowledgement of imperial fallibility and of Japan's inability to defend its territory. Japan had never been invaded; it had never been forced to grovel at the feet of a victorious foe. The calamity was greater than Westerners can imagine, for the surrender to the Allied forces was an admission that Japan's aspirations were overblown, its grasp too large, its confidence misplaced, and its future uncertain. Only a few short years before, Japanese armies had stormed triumphantly into China, Hong Kong, Singapore and the Philippines, and dared to drop bombs onto the airfields of Hawaii. The strutting Japanese forces had seemed invincible. Now, the evidence to the contrary was overwhelming. The act of surrender was a gesture of total supplication to the Americans, a capitulation of the civilian population as well as the military, a grudging abandonment of sovereignty.

In a transition as sweeping as Germany's rise from the chaos of World War I and the Weimar Republic into the ascendancy that sustained the launching of World War II, Japan was reborn. But it was not the same country; several defining characteristics had been stripped away. Bound by a new constitution (crafted by the Americans), this new nation was a decided step away from the militarism of the past. Whereas Germany reaped from the memory of war and the defeat of World War I the energy to rebuild and to regain its economic and military footing, Japan learned from the Pacific War the limits of military expansionism and the full impact of conquest. Relying again on its remarkable skills of adaptation and imitation, Japan set out to remake itself. And so it did, creating a remarkable industrial and financial empire that, in terms of power, outstripped the territorial gains and losses of World War II.

Canada stood back from this transformation, for it was of marginal importance on the international scene. Canada selected its roles carefully, attempting to emerge from Britain's imperial umbrella without being consumed by American protection. Using its flourishing diplomatic expertise—for which the country would become renowned in the 1950s and beyond—Canada assumed a position of moral and intellectual leadership, helping to found the United Nations (UN), assisting with the drafting of the UN Declaration of Human Rights and providing a model for First World countries in dealing with the emerging democracies of the former colonial world. This new role carried considerable prestige and accolades; however, it brought little real power and limited access to the international economy.

This was a crucial period for Canada in its relationship with Japan: the postwar era offered the country an opportunity to reestablish trade connections and to follow alongside Japan's remarkable economic surge. The years would quickly reveal this opportunity to be wasted, for Canadian government and business failed to understand the nature and speed of Japan's reconstruction and expansion. Content with the American-driven prosperity of the 1950s and 1960s and struggling with internal crises such as the issue of Quebec nationalism, Canadians did not set an ambitious agenda of international expansion, counting instead on traditional resource products to sustain the economy. Ironically, in an era when Canadian diplomats and peacekeepers gave the country an enviable international reputation, business and government failed to contribute. Ties with Japan remained, despite the obvious economic opportunities, largely uncultivated.

Japan After World War II

Japan's and Canada's positions could not have been more different than in 1945. Languishing, not victorious; occupied, not free; battered, not vibrant; demoralized, not buoyant; Japan faced immeasurable problems as it sought to rebuild. In the rubble of Tokyo, Hiroshima and Nagasaki lay the future of Japan, and only the most optimistic believed that the nation could rebound quickly. In the aftermath of the surrender, starvation and hardship ran through the land, adding to the sense of failure and hopelessness. The loss of over 2 million people (including 1 million civilians) during the war sucked the vitality out of the wartime generation and left Japan enfeebled.

The Japanese people recoiled against the memory of the war, sold as a nationalist and anti-imperialist crusade. The military heroes and the political leadership that had led the country to military disaster fell from their pedestals. Japan needed new directions, new leadership, and a new sense of national purpose. This sense of purpose came from the oddest of sources: the American-led occupation forces that took over the country after the armistice. Learning a lesson from World War I, when the anger and frustrations of the war carried over into postwar domination of the vanquished, the Allied powers sought to quickly integrate Japan and Germany into the western industrial mainstream and insisted on the immediate introduction of the structures, if not the values, of Western democracy.

It was the most unusual of partnerships. The Americans, led by the charismatic and domineering General MacArthur, shed the aggression of the war years and adopted the demeanour of a benign ally, sending millions of dollars to prop up the economy and maintain social order. The defeated Japanese did not conform to the wartime image of the crazed, suicidal fighters, an image developed by Allied countries, and they adapted quickly to occupation. The Japanese leadership cooperated freely with the Americans, and the people on the street seemingly harboured few grudges for the long and costly war; there was no apparent longing for the rulers who had drawn the country into the disastrous conflict.

Major changes came with astonishing rapidity. Japan was swiftly demilitarized; its soldiers constituted a reserve army of willing labour for the massive task of reconstruction. After Japanese officials failed to produce a suitable text, MacArthur appointed a team of Americans and instructed them to draft a new constitution in six days. The Constitution, implemented in May 1947, included such radical provisions as a renunciation of war, limits on the emperor's power, establishment of the Diet as the dominant political authority, and the enfranchisement of women. The constitution brought a wide variety of changes to labour rights, women's equality and judicial independence. Because the system integrated a variety of existing Japanese rules, procedures and values with a few Western imports, and because the Japanese were truly ready for a new order, the Constitution found a receptive, even enthusiastic, audience.

Japan's reconstruction had begun, but its path proved to be a long one. The new Japan, only scant years from a search for a military empire, would be built around liberal democracy, rapid reindustrialization and sweeping social change. The Americans believed that Japan would be recast in an American image, so sweeping was Japanese acceptance of the new order. But the Japan that reemerged from the ashes of war was truly Japanese in values, purpose and determination; the Western and liberal cast to the postwar period had largely picked up on a transition underway before the military interlude.

The Japanese economy stood at the centre of the country's redevelopment. Staggeringly high inflation—over 350 per cent in 1946 and not dropping under 20 per cent until 1950—complicated attempts to revitalize the economy. The government stepped in with strong measures: rationing, price restrictions and preferential treatment for key industries, particularly steel. The Allied occupation took other steps, breaking up the *zaibatsu* (groups of related large companies controlling large segments of the economy) in an attempt to increase competition and undertaking a major reform of landholding to democratize land ownership and agriculture. The Reconstruction Bank, created in 1947 to provide funds for desperately needed investment, did not stem inflationary pressures. The United States stepped in with the Dodge Plan of 1949, which fixed the yen's value relative to the American dollar and squeezed the government's budget. These stern measures worked, but at the cost of economic growth.

The glow faded from the occupation. Japan was getting back on its feet economically, though it had not returned to prewar standards. The rabid anticommunism of the United States troubled many in Japan, particularly when military bases in Japan (the Americans held Okinawa until 1972 and still maintain a military presence on the island) were used to launch the defence of South Korea in 1950. Within Japan, tensions between the Liberal Democratic Party (LDP) and the leftists unearthed both the vitality of the political process and the differences of opinion about the value of a continued American occupation. Negotiations followed, resulting in the 1951 treaties: a peace treaty and a treaty providing American protection in exchange for military bases in Japan. The American occupation ended, and Japan regained its independence on April 28, 1952.

The tasks facing postoccupation Japan were imposing indeed: reestablishing an international presence, planning for security in the tense Cold War era, regaining the trust of the Asian countries recently overrun by Japanese armies and creating a new economy. Japan's continued reliance on the United States for defence—a small self-defence force could scarcely protect the country—sparked mass protests and ongoing debate, particularly during the Vietnam War. The LDP maintained firm control over government, providing continuity through a period of constant change.

Japan was saved from potential difficulty by the sudden expansion of the Cold War, and particularly by the outbreak of war in Korea. Both a base and a primary supplier to the UN/American forces, Japan benefited tremendously from renewed East Asian militarization and suffered when the Korean conflict slowed. During this time, the United States saw Japan as a bulwark against Russian expansion, and made a concerted effort to keep Japan on side. Buttressed by American military spending, the economy grew strongly, from 6 to 9 per cent in the 1950s and from 6 to almost 14 per cent in the 1960s.

In 1960, Prime Minister Hayato Ikeda proclaimed that the country should aim to double personal income in a decade, a statement of seemingly staggering overconfidence. The critics were wrong, for the country hit its target within seven years. Japan's prosperity rested on a series of interrelated factors: low prices for imported raw materials, solid government guidance and a very high savings rate, which provided the money necessary to invest in new and updated industries. The Japanese postponed individual prosperity and instant consumer gratification in the interest of building Japan's economy. The country made massive investments in infrastructure and industrial development, providing a remarkably firm foundation for long-term growth; Japan, unlike Canada, did not borrow internationally to pay for the cost of building the economy.

Japan's economic growth was far from happenstance. The national government played a major role, largely through the banking industry and the Ministry of International Trade and Industry (MITI). Long-range, regularly updated plans provided investors and businesses with projections for future development. As well, the government targeted key industries for special treatment, typically in the form of loans or access to foreign exchange, and encouraged investment in new technologies or the development of new markets. The interaction between government and business in Japan was unique, far from the suspicion-riddled protectionist and regulation-oriented Canadian system and the *laissez-faire* American approach, and it served the country exceptionally well in this period of rapid industrialization and economic globalization. Economists described Japan as a capitalist development state, highlighting the role of government in crafting economic policy; most observers simply called it a miracle.

The expansion burst in the early 1970s. Problems with an undervalued yen and an overvalued American dollar convinced the government of the United States to let the dollar float in 1973, causing drastic increases in the value of the yen and the cost of Japanese exports. A more serious shock followed that same year, when the OPEC (Organization of Petrolium Exporting Countries) oil embargo hit Japanese industry severely and touched off an inflationary frenzy. (President Richard Nixon's reconciliation visit to China in 1972, undertaken without consultation with Japan, touched off similar consternation, for it demonstrated to Japan just how isolated it was from the United States.) Japan's growth rate slowed dramatically through the 1970s, due to the oil shock (including a second oil crisis in 1979–80), which coincided with a drop in investment and a lessening of the pace of technological innovation. Japan's miracle ended, although the country remained prosperous and internationally important. At the same time, the Japanese discovered the negative consequences of almost unbridled industrial development, and turned their attentions to improving the quality of the Japanese environment.

The end of the Japanese miracle did not signal the economic collapse forecast by Western observers. Japan entered a period of slower growth, but continued its fascinating pattern of market development. However, another problem loomed. In the early 1980s, Japan established a sizeable trade surplus with the United States, much to the Americans' chagrin. When the Japanese yen, sitting at around 220 to 230 yen per dollar, began to depreciate (rather than appreciate, as experts anticipated), Japanese imports declined in cost and increased in attractiveness. The Americans demanded action, and blamed Japan's restrictive trading policies for its burgeoning trade surplus with their country. In September 1985, representatives of five major trading nations—the United States, Japan, Germany, the

United Kingdom and France—gathered in New York City and struck a deal, called the Plaza Accord, to push down the value of the American dollar. Markets responded rapidly, with the yen rising to 150 yen per dollar within nine months. The establishment of the Plaza Accord signalled a new era for the Japanese economy, a period in which its internal policies and global activities faced increased international scrutiny. Japan's success, and the fact that it had worked its way to a dominant international trading position, created resentment and resulted in numerous attempts by other countries to replicate the achievement.

The manifestations of Japan's reemergence were truly remarkable, for no country in the world had ever experienced such steady economic expansion. Consumerism swept across the land, reaching into the most isolated corners of the country and helping to break the historical distinction between the modernized cities and the traditional farming districts. When the rest of the world visited for the Tokyo Olympic Games in 1964, Japan offered nothing less spectacular than rebuilt cities, a vibrant economy and a wealthy, industrialized society. The country had stabilized, displaying unity and strength that few other nations could match, relying on economic success to smooth out any differences within the land.

Perhaps more important, Japan established a new international image. The old stereotype of military fanaticism was suppressed, but it has not disappeared, aided by the Japanese refusal until August 1995 to formally acknowledge and apologize for its wartime atrocities. Japan's new image consists of crafty businessmen, cunning traders and dedicated workers. Billions of dollars worth of Japanese trinkets—cheap goods, often imitations of more expensive American products—found their way onto world markets. Japan traded with the world, penetrating the sensitive American market, but not forgetting the importance of trade to East Asia and Europe.

Japan managed the transition from poverty to wealth, from devastation to industrial power, with remarkable acuity. Elsewhere, rapid economic growth was matched by social and political unrest, but Japan escaped this turmoil. The flood of thousands into the major cities was not followed by increased crime or internal tensions, as it was in the United States and Canada. The education system, which had expanded rapidly in the occupation years, proved integral to the economic revival, spurring students on to greater achievements. Education assumed national importance, emerging as the pride of Japan and the key to continued success.

This was a Japan that few had expected to see within a century, let alone twenty years, of the end of the war. By the early 1970s, the country was confident, nationalistic in a nonmilitary manner, and sure of its natural ascendancy on the world stage. Success carried problems, including urban crowding, environmental degradation and international resentment of the country's sky-rocketing prosperity. Japan did not react well to criticisms, particularly from the Americans, who resented Japan's continued expansion (and the emerging domination of the electronics and automobile industries). But it was impossible not to be impressed, for Japan had succeeded when few believed it could. To rise from postwar devastation and become one of the world's great trading nations in little over twenty years stands as one of the greatest achievements of this century.

Pacific Diplomacy

Canada was, in the 1950s, still a bit player on the international stage. That a Canadian diplomat (and later prime minister), Lester B. Pearson, won the Nobel Peace Prize for orchestrating UN intervention in the Suez crisis of 1956 confirmed the country's role as a diplomatic middle power, straddling the line between First and Third Worlds. But Canada was preoccupied with internal development and the exploitation of its seemingly inexhaustible supplies of raw materials. With the voracious American economy to the south, there was little need to look further afield for markets, or to develop more creative links to other national economies.

However, the Canadian public resented Prime Minister King's goal of increasing the continentalism of the nation's economy, as well as the weakening of the British connection. In the 1950s, the country was very much a British Dominion and an active participant in the Commonwealth, to a degree that Canadians of the 1990s would find surprising and a bit humorous. The British tie had brought the Dominion of Canada into existence and to a reasonable level of prosperity; most Canadians wanted this connection maintained, if not expanded. But the British lion was, by the postwar period, tired and ravaged, its international presence and significance declining by the year. Much as Canadians wanted to enhance their relationship with Britain, and thus avoid further entanglement with the more boisterous, domineering United States, economic and political realities dictated that Canada move further down that path.

Japan, indeed the entire Pacific region, played only a minor role in Canadian plans during this period, and both nations did little to improve their relationship for twenty years after the war. In Canada, as in America, racism had flourished during the war, and the signing of the peace accords did not quickly eliminate the deeply ingrained hostilities; memories of Hong Kong and prison-camp atrocities remained alive in the minds of many Canadians. Canada was also struggling to come to terms with its treatment of Japanese Canadians during the war. Although these citizens had gained the right to vote in 1947, they were also actively encouraged to return to Japan after the surrender. Japanese-Canadian demands for compensation were only partly met; most claimants had to settle for a small percentage of the actual value of confiscated property. There was no great Canadian desire to reach out across the Pacific in harmony and partnership, and some Canadians even expressed frustration that the costs of defeat were not more pronounced. The federal government conducted a liaison mission and reestablished a diplomatic presence in Japan after the war, but took few other steps.

In the mid-1950s, Canada lost one of its foremost authorities on Japan. Herbert Norman, born in Japan to missionary parents, worked for the Department of External Affairs in the country of his birth before World War II and returned with the Allied occupation force after the war. Norman was greatly admired by the Japanese, and he wrote extensively about the country and its economic potential. His casual associations with left-wing movements as a student came back to haunt him in the Cold War atmosphere of the 1950s, when questions were raised about his loyalty and suitability for sensitive government postings. The Canadian government, having investigated his past, sided with the accomplished diplomat and scholar, and moved him to a post in Egypt. But the Americans, pursuing communists under every conceivable bed, kept after Norman, eventually publicizing his former left-wing affiliations. Distraught by the intense scrutiny (Norman was never a security risk in his professional duties), Canada's leading expert on Japan committed suicide in 1957. Norman's death, which Canadian officials blamed on American excess, stimulated anti-American sentiments in Canada; in Japan, the loss of one of the most sensitive Western analysts of the country was equally mourned. (Norman was one of the more influential Westerners in Japan in the mid-twentieth century, and his writing attracts a strong intellectual following to this day.)

Economics, not a search for a cultural partnership, stood behind the expansion of Canadian-Japanese relations. Japan's historic ties to the Canadian resource sector, combined with the demands from a rapidly growing industrial economy, ensured that the trade links between the two countries would be reestablished and then expanded. And grow they did, albeit in the traditional markets and with relatively little assistance on the part of the Canadian government or business community. Japan was distant, distinctive and still very exotic; Canadian companies were pleased to sell their products in the Japanese market, provided the price was right and the Japanese took the lead in identifying the need. And so it was essentially Japanese instigation that rebuilt the prewar trading connections and formed the base for expanded trade as Japan's needs increased and as Canadian resources came available.

Until the 1970s, Canada made few efforts to make Japan the focus of its diplomatic agenda. Canada's highly regarded diplomatic corps helped Japan find acceptance among Western nations and earned Japan's lasting friendship as a result. However, Japan did not find a great deal of value or importance in Canada. Relations between the countries focused almost exclusively on trade matters (although the Canadian government opened an immigration office in Japan in 1967). The Canadian government's primary task during this time was to ensure that the United States gave priority to Canadian matters. This task proved challenging, given President Nixon's belief that Japan was a more important trading partner than Canada. Japan, preoccupied with a rapidly expanding economy, gave Canada polite but detached attention, also having more important gardens to tend. As had been the case for much of the twentieth century, Canada continued to struggle for international recognition and acceptance.

Limited American interest in Canada, coupled with the realization of the country's increasing dependence on the American economy, convinced the Trudeau administration to consider other approaches. In the early 1970s, Prime Minister Trudeau and Mitchell Sharp, the minister of external affairs, developed the "third option," a strategy for expansion of Canadian economic and diplomatic contacts with the European Community and Japan. (The first option was to maintain Canada's current relationship with the United States; the second was to seek greater integration with the American economy.) For the first time, Canada made a visible effort to reach out to Japan, while seeking to strengthen contacts with Europe. A strong personal relationship between Prime Minister Trudeau and Yasuhiko Nara, Japanese ambassador to Canada, facilitated the new initiative, resulting in the negotiation of the Framework for Economic Cooperation in 1976. As had happened before and would happen again, Canada and

Japan declared their mutual desire to enhance trade; putting these diplomatic words into action was another matter. The Trudeau initiative exemplifies the potential for and the barriers to Canada-Japan interaction. Historians Norman Hillmer and Jack Granatstein, reviewing the two-pronged effort to enhance trade with Europe and Japan, concluded:

> The government's trade bureaucracy considered the links a daydream, flying in the face of geographical reality. Almost no one at the Department of Trade and Commerce took them seriously and neither did their business clients. Deterred by the difficulties of fighting for business in multilingual Europe, Canadian companies hung back, and the intricacies of Japanese culture simply baffled them. Trade figures with Japan increased to $5.3 billion in exports and imports combined, but the grand words about co-operation proved meaningless...It was very hard to reverse established patterns. Trudeau had tried, but ultimately he, or rather his bureaucracy and Canadian business, had failed (*Empire to Umpire: Canada and the World to the 1990s*, pp. 301–302).

Within the next decade, evidence accumulated that the highly publicized diplomatic accords, particularly Trudeau and Nara's framework, had produced little substantive change in Canada-Japan relations. Similar Canadian efforts followed in the Mulroney administration (1984–93), but once again the civil service and the Canadian business community put little substance into the political rhetoric. Canadians, and the federal government, gradually abandoned the third option in favour of increased continental integration, taking sides on a Canadian dilemma that extends back into the nineteenth century. The result was NAFTA, a blazingly clear sign that Canada has tied its economic horse to the American wagon train. Thus, it is not surprising that, as Klaus Pringsheim, President of the Canada-Japan Trade Council, concluded, "Japan remains unwilling to regard Canada as anything more than a resource hinterland of the United States and is as yet not disposed to consider Canada as a major potential supplier of manufactured and processed goods for the Japanese market, nor as a sophisticated industrial nation, distinct and separate from the United States" (*Neighbours across the Pacific*, pp. 195–196).

Still-Distant Neighbours

Several decades of diplomatic relations and strong, growing trade connections brought Canada and Japan closer together, but great distances remain. Both nations made a greater effort to understand the other. Japanese scholars established the Japanese Association for Canadian Studies, with financial support from Canada; Canadian academics, backed by the Japanese government and private sector agencies, created the Japan Studies Association of Canada. Academic exchanges, conferences and undergraduate programs (small Canadian Studies programs in Japan and comprehensive East Asian Studies programs in Canada) emerged out of these relationships. Nevertheless, relatively few Japanese scholars have undertaken extensive research in Canada, and the high (and escalating) cost of conducting research in Japan has undercut the efforts of Canadian academics.

International media links have brought more news of Japan to Canadians; the 1994 Kobe earthquake was covered extensively by news channels, which provided updates on developments in the devastated city. However, few reports were presented from a Canadian perspective. Canadian media send reporters to Japan during major events and Canadian diplomatic excursions, but only Southam News' Andrew Horvath gives systematic coverage. A Tokyo daily newspaper, Nihon Keizai Shimbun, has a staff reporter based in Toronto, focusing largely on business affairs and providing Japan with a small flow of information from Canada.

On a more personal level, tourist travel has provided people on both sides of the Pacific with an opportunity to experience the other country. The Japanese have been truly fascinated with Canada, particularly Prince Edward Island (due to the Japanese love of the Anne of Green Gables stories), the West Coast and the Rocky Mountain National Parks of Banff and Jasper. In 1993, over 400,000 Japanese visitors came to Canada and a paltry 73,000 Canadians travelled to Japan. In the same year, over 25,000 Japanese lived in Canada (more than 14,000 as permanent residents). It is questionable how much of Canada Japanese tourists actually see, for the vast majority travel in groups on Japanese-managed tours. Of course, the same is true of most Canadian tourists visiting Japan, for language and cultural barriers make independent travel difficult for most visitors.

A handful of Canadian communities have attempted to create stronger ties with Japan through sister-city relationships. Often dismissed as boondoggles for civic officials, sister-city arrangements can strengthen commercial and personal relationships and form the foundation for lasting cultural and business exchanges. Historically, Canadian cities have sought connections with American communities and, particularly in Quebec and New Brunswick, with cities in France. Beginning in the 1970s, as Canadians came to realize the current and potential significance of Japan, efforts to establish municipal connections expanded markedly, from less than 15 pairings in 1975 to 53 in 1993. The Canadian partners came primarily from three provinces: British Columbia, Alberta and Ontario. Quebec has no sister city relationships with Japan and the Maritimes only one (Halifax and Hakodate).

While many of the sister-city connections are inactive or merely ceremonial, some of the more active relationships have been very successful. Alberta's efforts to actively promote arrangements with Hokkaido are credited with increasing Alberta beef sales and encouraging investment in the Bank of Alberta. Cambridge, Ontario, site of the massive Toyota plant, twinned with Toyota City in an effort to further economic and technological exchange. Quesnel, British Columbia, has an active relationship with Shiraoi that is built on commercial connections relating to the pulp and paper industry. Kariya helped construct the Kariya Japanese garden in the downtown area of its partner, Mississauga, Ontario; the garden serves as a strong visual reminder of the partnership. In British Columbia, Campbell River's twinning with Ishikari originated with Japanese investment in a local mill, and helped encourage both further investment and Japanese purchase of local mill products. The primary emphasis of the sister-city arrangements remains on building business and commercial links, and using twinning to overcome some of the obvious cultural and social barriers to successful interaction.

There are other formal initiatives, such as the Asia Pacific Foundation, the Canada-Japan Businessmen's Conference and the Canada-Japan Trade Council, and short-term undertakings, including the Canada-Japan Forum 2000, a bilateral panel co-chaired by former Alberta premier Peter Lougheed and Yoshio Okawara, designed to bring the two countries closer together. Most of these initiatives begin with commercial considerations, and have as a primary objective helping to overcome the cultural and social gap between Canada and Japan. While the participants, active in Canada-Japan trade, are sincerely interested in expanding contacts, it is unlikely that this approach will find more than modest success.

Organizational cooperation, like government-led initiatives, does not spring from a genuine Canadian desire to understand Japan (and vice versa) and does not reflect the minor level of internationalism within the Canadian body politic. The Japanese do not understand Canada well, but they learn a great deal about the United States. Most Japanese see Canada as an underdeveloped frontier of the United States; this limited level of understanding is cause for concern. The Japanese, intensely proud of their national accomplishments, nonetheless know that they must forge their way in a competitive, complex and increasingly interrelated world. Canadians, conversely, lack a strong sense of accomplishment and commitment to their country and have virtually opted out of the international race. In today's globalized economy, Canada's approach to Japan is symptomatic of a nation that has turned its back on the ways of a rapidly changing world.

***

Fifty years have passed since the end of World War II, and it is a testament to that armed struggle's remarkable impact that the war finds itself, yet again, in the news. While Canadians have enjoyed a victor's remembrance of battle, Japan continues to wrestle with its World War II legacy. Through the summer of 1995, as a prelude to the fiftieth anniversary of the end of the war in the Pacific, Japanese politicians debated bitterly the proper way to acknowledge Japan's actions. Many Japanese, including then Prime Minister Tomichi Murayama, supported formal apologies for the war and for acts of brutality toward conquered countries. A conservative backlash greeted the proposals for a War Apology Resolution and, for a time, threatened to bring down Murayama's government. Although it became clear that the public supported some form of expression of regret (remembering that for decades Japanese school children learned very little about the war), the final statement stopped short of a full apology to the countries occupied during the war. Instead, Japan's cabinet agreed to express its sincere regret for the excesses of Japanese aggression.

This long-awaited recognition is designed primarily for Asian consumption, for the string of countries—Hong Kong, China, Singapore, the Philippines and Indonesia—that have very bitter memories of Japan's wartime occupation. These nations have recently emerged as major trading partners and may well hold the key to Japanese prosperity in the next century. The apology, then, is more than a simple expiation for past wrongs; it is a means of tying up moral and historical loose ends. With the statement of apology, Japan hopes to turn the final page on World War II and redirect the country and its neighbours toward the next century.

5

The Changing Face of Canadian and Japanese Societies

Although Japan's economic success and, at least within Canada, Canada's economic woes, attract great attention, the social and cultural underpinnings of these societies remain uninvestigated. As Japan and Canada turn to the challenges of the twenty-first century, they will find their options constrained by their past and their opportunities conditioned by their culture. Foreign observers of Japan, deflected by the intricacies of the Japanese language and culture, typically focus on the perceived eccentricities of the country and its people. A deeper examination, however, reveals the degree to which Japan's national successes, and its failings, are deeply rooted in the country's social make-up. Similarly, as Canadians seek to understand their options for the future, they must focus on the constraints and foundations established by the nation's heritage, values and cultural assumptions.

Only rarely in the history of the world have societies faced as many baffling, complex and interrelated changes as they do in the late twentieth century. Conservatives wax eloquently about the "old days": times of fixed social conventions, commonly shared values and acceptance of established authority. But such nostalgic renderings of the past neither do justice to history nor provide a suitable foundation for facing the future. Given the rapid pace of contemporary social change, which is largely related to overcoming distance and cultural barriers through modern communications technologies, it is easy to understand the attraction in both Canada and Japan of returning to family values and traditional ways of living.

These are troubling, difficult times, and the next few decades remain shrouded in uncertainty. The crush of environmental pressures, urbanization, generational conflicts, and economic transition has fuelled tremendous dissatisfaction with the political process and created an open contest for the hearts and minds of Canadians and Japanese alike. Allegiances appear less important than they were in the 1970s, existing value systems face new and repeated attacks, and globalized pop culture makes continued inroads into national cultural traditions.

Canada and Japan approach the complexity and turmoil of the late twentieth century from radically different starting points. In addition to the obvious ethnic difference (an Asian nation versus a predominantly European society), fundamental differences explain both the contemporary social systems and the abilities of these two nations to meet the striking social challenges that lie ahead. The present circumstances offer a test of national core values and of the willingness and capacity of each country to tackle future problems. How the countries deal with contemporary difficulties and respond to the opportunities of the next century is substantially determined by their cultural and social characteristics.

These countries are not similar, although the size of the gap is magnified by social distance and linguistic barriers. Canada is not about to adopt most of Japan's cultural norms, just as Japan is clearly in no rush to copy North American standards. The effort to enhance commercial, diplomatic and cultural relations, however, must rest on a more advanced understanding of the differences and similarities between the two nations.

Understanding the "Other"

Westerners have, since the nineteenth century, struggled to understand and explain Japan. Bookshelves are full of volumes seeking to describe Japan's society and culture; some are insightful, many are ethnocentric and others are simply ill informed. Recent books are more comprehensive than early-twentieth-century offerings, but the occasional work retains the mocking tone that has occasionally infiltrated Western attempts to comprehend the Land of the Rising Sun. As well, Western writers tend to fall into one of two camps: either Japan is a miracle, with no serious weaknesses, or Japan is fraught with internal contradictions and difficulties and has managed to mask its national failings from Western eyes. A smaller group adopts a more balanced approach, acknowledging Japan's accomplishments and strengths while recognizing that some of these successes exact a price and suggesting that the nation, like most others, faces serious challenges in the years ahead.

In Canada's case, it is not that outsiders have failed to properly describe the country's social and cultural make-up; rather, it is that very few have tried (Andrew Malcolm, who wrote *The Canadians*, is one of these few). The nation still awaits its de Tocqueville, the nineteenth-century French writer who so brilliantly described the roots of American society and culture. Canada is either too bland to attract notice or too easy to explain; the country is deemed to be too much like the United States to warrant attention, or it is judged to be unworthy of consideration. Japan, on the other hand, remains hidden behind a veil of Asian complexity.

Japan: A Social Explanation

Remembering Japan's history helps us understand many of the deeply ingrained characteristics of the Japanese people. There are several key elements to this history: the mythology, which holds that the Japanese are a divine race and that their imperial line descends directly from the sun goddess, Amaterasu; the 250 years of the Tokugawa period in which Japan was almost completely closed to the outside world; and the beginning of the Meiji era, when Japan struggled to catch up to the West and be accepted as an equal power. Each of these developments greatly influenced the growth of the nation, fostered a strong sense of national identity and enhanced feelings of uniqueness.

Japan is one of the most homogeneous and most exclusive societies on earth: 99.4 per cent of Japan's population is Japanese, 0.5 per cent is Korean and 0.1 per cent consists of other races, primarily the Chinese. In some respects, this exclusivity borders on the extreme. For example, Koreans whose ancestors were first brought to Japan during the Japanese occupation of Korea (1910–45) and who have lived all their lives in Japan are still required to carry alien registration cards, like all non-Japanese residents. These residents often speak only Japanese, have Japanese names and are physically indistinguishable from the native Japanese. Until 1993, fingerprints were also mandatory, but after considerable pressure from Seoul, this requirement was finally dropped for permanent residents. (It is interesting to note that the approximately 600,000 Koreans in Japan include numerous North Korean sympathizers who provide substantial funds for the North. The United States has been pressuring Japan to clamp down on the repatriation of monies to stop this flow of money to North Korea, but it has so far been unsuccessful.)

"To be Japanese," wrote John Condon in *With Respect to the Japanese*, "is to be born of Japanese parents, to look Japanese, to speak Japanese, and to act Japanese—the full set. Change any part and you spoil the symmetry, like a sour note in a sonata" (Condon, *With Respect*, Introduction). Even Japanese people who live abroad for a number of years often feel that they cannot fit into society when they return home. Reassimilation can be so difficult that support groups have sprung up to help people returning to Japan after living abroad.

Much of this feeling of displacement stems from the Japanese concepts of *uchi* (inside) and *soto* (outside). Clear distinctions between the inside and the outside permeate Japanese society, beginning with the clean inside of the house and the dirty outside world. Entrances to all Japanese homes have a *genkan*, a porch where guests discard shoes and outside dirt before entering the house. The Japanese have ritualized sayings for crossing the *genkan* into or out of the house. The inside, whether referring to the house or to a group of people, is safe and secure; the outside is unpredictable and frightening. Speech and behaviour are determined by whom one is with and by whether or not that person is part of one's group (inside). This explains why the Japanese can be exceedingly polite with friends and colleagues but pushy and rude when in crowds or with strangers. *Uchi* varies depending on the circumstances: in certain situations, one's *uchi* group is the extended family or the company; at other times, the *uchi* group is Japan and the rest of the world is *soto*, or outside. While Japan welcomes visitors, especially from North America and Europe, it is difficult, if not impossible, for them to become fully assimilated into Japanese society. The word for foreigner in Japanese, *gaijin*, is literally translated as "outside person," and foreign residents often feel this sense of "outsideness." And although the Japanese are generally impressed by foreigners who have made an effort to learn the language and to become familiar with customs and culture, they are uncomfortable with foreigners who become "too Japanese."

Given this preoccupation with distinctiveness, it is hardly surprising to discover that the Japanese are passionately interested in themselves. Books on *Nihonjin-ron* (Japan theory) discuss the special attributes of the Japanese, those characteristics which presumably distinguish them from other people. Robert Christopher, author of *The Japanese Mind* and long-time Japan reporter for *Newsweek*, commented, "Convinced, accurately enough, of the uniqueness of their culture, the Japanese also like to think that it is so subtle and complex that no one who was not born Japanese and reared in Japanese society can ever truly become a part of it" (p. 186). Even today, many Japanese are amazed to find foreigners who like sushi or who can say a few words in Japanese. North Americans residing for a long time in Japan often remark that they will scream if asked one more time about their ability with chopsticks. The Japanese sense of uniqueness sometimes reaches absurd proportions. An article in the *Japan Times* quoted a Japanese doctor as stating that Japanese women's hips are flatter than foreign women's and that this physiology facilitates giving birth. It has been claimed that the Japanese cannot learn to speak English because their mouths are different, and that Japan should not import skis because Japanese snow is unlike any other snow in the world. These ideas are not the domain of fringe elements. No less an authority than former Prime Minister Tsutomu Hata, speaking as the minister of agriculture, claimed that Western beef should not be imported into the country because the intestines of Japanese people had difficulty digesting foreign meat.

The Japanese Language

Language is another barrier to Japan's relationship with the rest of the world. The Japanese language is not closely related to any other language although it is classified in the Altaic family along with Korean, Mongolian and Turkish. In the sixth century, the Japanese borrowed Chinese pictographs for their written language; this was an interesting decision, given that the two languages are grammatically extremely dissimilar. Japanese uses these Chinese characters or kanji, but to cope with inflection, verb endings and foreign words (among other things), it also uses two phonetic alphabets. To complete the nine years of compulsory education, students must know 1,945 kanji. With that number, they can make their way through a Japanese newspaper, but they would need to know additional characters if they wished to read anything more scholarly. Learning kanji is a time-consuming and difficult task, as many characters have more than ten strokes (and some have as many as forty). Almost all characters have more than one pronunciation—one drawn from Chinese, and the rest, native Japanese words, which are similar in meaning to the original Chinese pictograph. Equally challenging is understanding honorifics in Japanese. These are the polite forms used in conversation with someone considered to be of higher social status. Basically, the verb forms change depending upon the speaker's relationship to the person being spoken to. With all these complications, it is easy to understand why Saint Francis Xavier, the sixteenth-century Spanish Jesuit missionary to Japan, called Japanese "the devil's language."

Structure in Japanese Society

The natural order in Japan includes a strong emphasis on status and rank differentiation. People adjust their language and their behaviour depending on the rank of the person with whom they are interacting. This pattern, strikingly at odds with Western egalitarian thought, has its roots in the feudal and Confucian Tokugawan society, and remains strong to the present day. However, position and status were inherited in Tokugawan times. Today, except in the case of some traditional arts, the Japanese must work to achieve positions of prestige. Generally, the status of the individual's organization (corporation or university) determines personal standing in society; a lower position in a large, prestigious corporation carries a higher status than a higher position in a smaller, less famous company. Within schools and companies, rank is strongly related to age and length of time in the organization. Those who enter a company in any given year at the same level (that is, blue-collar or white-collar) in any given year form a class, *dōki* (same period), and members of this class stay closely in step in both rank and salary for most of their careers. Those who joined the company (or the school or the swim team) earlier are referred to as *sempai* (senior, superior or elder) by those who joined later. A *sempai* is responsible for looking out for and mentoring those below him or her. In return, the *kohai* (junior) respects and obeys the *sempai*. (In practical terms, this means that a *kohai* follows the *sempai's* orders—for example, *kohai* in sports clubs set up and take down all equipment—and that the *sempai* pays for meals and other activities for the *kohai*.)

As per Confucian teachings, within families, older children are higher than younger children, boys are higher than girls, fathers are higher than mothers. Although these status differences are not as important as they once were, they still exist. The Japanese almost always specify if a sibling is younger or older, and siblings refer to each other not by name, but by rank—as *oneesan* (older sister), for example. The eldest son in a Japanese family carries certain responsibilities, such as looking after his parents in their old age or continuing the family business, and he receives certain benefits, including inheriting the family home. When it is time for family members to have their bath (*ofuro*) before bed, everyone soaks in the same hot water (after washing outside the tub), bathing in order of seniority.

The Japanese generally accept the authority of hierarchy and follow its rules easily. In fact, the Japanese are uncomfortable with those who do not act according to their age and position. Challenging the order of status on either side—bosses who are casual and informal or students who argue with their professors—is embarrassing and awkward for the Japanese. Because hierarchy is valued so highly, relations of equality are relatively rare.

A Middle-Class Society

Despite this emphasis on hierarchy, the Japanese do not have a strong sense of class and class difference. The vast majority of Japanese, until fairly recently about 90 per cent, consider themselves to be middle-class, a perception that accords with fiscal realities. There are no large groups of extremely wealthy or extremely poor people in Japan. (A simple look around a subway car or a crowded street invariably reveals a well-dressed, clean and healthy-looking population. With the exception of the main train stations in Tokyo and Osaka, evidence of poverty or despair is difficult to find, and expensive homes often sit right beside much more modest accommodations.) One sign of the comparative lack of class differentiation is the gap in salaries paid to employees at the bottom and at the top of the corporate ladder. While North American company presidents draw million-dollar salaries, earning many times more than the workers in their firms, Japanese executives, even in some of the world's largest industrial firms, take home only seven times the average worker's salary.

However, the astronomical cost of housing and land is beginning to divide Japanese society into those who do and those who do not own property. Average white-collar workers in major Japanese cities can no longer realize their dream of owning a living space that would be considered minimally acceptable in Canada. Many Japanese families live in small apartments consisting of two or three small rooms, a kitchen with an eating area and a bathroom. For those urbanites who do not inherit property or receive low-cost loans from their employers, owning a home is unlikely. If they are able to purchase something, it will not be very large, and it will most likely be a long commute from the office in the city. (Particularly in Tokyo, even apartment dwellers often commute two to three hours daily.) Many

Japanese feel bitter about their living conditions and wonder aloud about Japan's economic prosperity, when they are living and working in conditions far inferior to those of peoples of supposedly less prosperous nations. One simple comparison puts the value of Japanese real estate in stark perspective: at the height of the Japanese real estate boom, the estimated value of the Imperial Palace grounds in downtown Tokyo equalled the value of all of the real estate in Canada!

Small living quarters have a dramatic effect on the lives of their inhabitants. Traditionally, elderly Japanese people lived with their children and grandchildren, but cramped living conditions have made this arrangement difficult, and the numbers of elderly people living with their families are decreasing. Children who live in apartments or homes with tiny yards must play in public playgrounds, and some adults seeking peace and quiet rent private reading rooms by the month. The Japanese seldom entertain at home, instead meeting friends in coffee shops or restaurants. The lack of privacy in these small homes means that married couples anxious for time alone often patronize Japan's many "love hotels." Clearly, fewer activities are taking place at home, thus changing the dynamics of domestic life.

The Group in Japanese Life

Japanese society tends to value the group over the individual, and children learn this value right from birth. Jared Taylor, author of *Shadows of the Rising Sun*, explains that "in Japan, the baby is considered an independent organism that must be drawn into the bosom of the family in an increasingly dependent way for it to mature. In America the baby is seen as a dependent creature that must be taught to stand alone" (p. 169). This fundamental difference is reflected in child-rearing techniques: Japanese infants and small children are almost never left alone, and they often sleep in their parents' bed until they are five or six years old. Even when children are older, they tend to sleep in rooms with other people, rather than in individual rooms. Small children grow up in a permissive environment and develop an expectation of understanding indulgence from their mothers. They are more likely to be disciplined by exclusion from family activities than by any other means. All of these practices encourage a dependence on the family group rather than a sense of individuality and independence.

Most Japanese people are more content than the average Westerner to conform in the way they dress, act and live. Society places a higher value on team players than on others who, though possibly brighter or more talented, are more individualistic or independent-minded. As the old Japanese saying goes, "The nail that sticks up gets pounded down." Few students pursue graduate degrees, as employers prefer to hire generalists and train them in the corporate mould. Group affiliations are very important, and the Japanese often identify themselves first by their company or university and then by their own name. Group hiking, skiing or picnicking expeditions are much more common than private outings: even group honeymoons are fairly popular. Office workers will, after being at work, day and night, six days in a row, readily agree, in most cases without resentment to spend Sunday at a company picnic. Uniforms, company or school songs and formally structured activities enhance the participants' sense of belonging.

This emphasis on the group affects Japanese interpersonal relations. For groups to operate successfully, members must work to preserve harmony and avoid conflict. Public displays of strong emotions, such as anger or love, elicit negative reactions. The Japanese will often go to great lengths to preserve harmony. There is a desire to minimize embarrassment and a reluctance to say "no" directly; a myriad of ways exist to indicate disagreement without explicitly saying so (a vital point that Westerners, particularly business people, often miss). The Japanese often use go-betweens to allow involved parties to express their views without the danger of confrontation or loss of face. They take much more responsibility than Westerners for the behaviour of members of their group or family. One member's disgrace is shared by everyone, which gives the group strong reasons for preventing its members from misbehaving. When a corporate scandal occurs, all employees of that company feel a sense of responsibility for the incident and would go to great lengths to protect the honour of the company. As Jared Taylor reports in *Shadows of the Rising Sun*, Japan's

> sense of national cohesion is a built-in extension of group loyalty. With loyalty to the national group comes a broad and touching sense of responsibility. A few years ago an American journalist wrote: "If the theft of a camera from an alien is reported in the newspapers, the amazed foreigner may find himself presented with several replacements by Japanese who are complete strangers but who feel that the stain caused to the community reputation must be erased." Even a thief is part of a national group; his actions implicate all Japanese (p. 86).

The Japanese speak of *tatemae*, best translated as outward appearance, the formal answer or the facade, and *honne*, meaning genuine motives or true feelings. Clearly understood rules determine when each mode of behaviour is appropriate. For Westerners, the Japanese use of *tatemae* and the tendency toward vagueness and insinuation, rather than direct statements, can be confusing and frustrating. (Some of these traits are not as alien as they first appear; for example, Canadians, in an effort to be polite, often compliment someone on a new hairstyle or piece of clothing they do not necessarily like.)

The Costs and Benefits of the Japanese Education System

In Japan, educational guidelines are fairly well laid out, and they are inculcated at an early age. As Ken Schoolland comments in *Shogun's Ghost: The Dark Side of Japanese Education*, "One thing stands out: young people are viewed as a national resource. As such, the young are intended to serve some national purpose. This is usually, but not always, a national economic purpose" (p. 9). The education system is the primary means of indoctrinating Japanese children into the ways of the nation, and it provides an excellent insight into the rigidities and the strengths of Japanese society.

In order to produce students and then adults with the desired qualifications, Japan's education system is tightly organized. Students across the nation, from Okinawa to Hokkaido, study the same material on the same day. Although local school boards may decide which textbooks to use, they make their choices from a limited list of books compiled by the ministry of education. The subjects taught in all elementary and junior high schools and the tiniest details of each course are determined by the ministry. Teachers have some flexibility as to how they teach but none whatsoever regarding what they teach. An example of this rigidity is the controversial battle waged by Saburo Ienaga, a former professor at Tokyo University, against the government for forcing him to delete references in his textbooks to the brutality of Japan's invasion of China. For example, Ienaga was forced to change "Japan's invasion of China" to "Japan's advancement into China." This case has been before the courts since 1967, and so far, the courts have always ruled in the ministry's favour.

On a purely functional level, Japanese children are among the best educated in the world. Virtually all Japanese children graduate from junior high and over 90 per cent complete high school. Despite the extreme complexity of the Japanese writing system, the illiteracy rate is less than 1 per cent. The Japanese school year is substantially longer than the Canadian school year (240 days, compared to 180 days), the school week is a half day longer (including Saturday mornings) and the actual school day is longer. Japanese children are assigned substantial amounts of homework, even during the summer holidays; primary students are required to do a minimum of one to two hours of school work daily. Although the types of classes required are very similar to those required in Canada, the expected degree of mastery is often greater than that demanded of Canadian children. Japanese children score extremely high, often ranking first in the world, on international math and science examinations. However, that Japanese students score well on tests is not necessarily surprising, for this is what the school system trains them to do. The system's weakness lies in its lack of attention to learning beyond memorization. Students are not trained to ask questions, express opinions, write essays or think for themselves. Classes are large (often over forty students), and attention to individual strengths and weaknesses is therefore difficult, if not impossible.

At almost all public schools, children wear uniforms, and strict conformity is enforced for almost all aspects of a child's life, from hairstyles (no perms, hair dyes or unusual cuts) to behaviour off the school grounds. Teachers become involved in students' lives to a degree that would be construed as meddling in Canada. Teachers telephone mothers if children violate any of the rules, and they drop by to see if students are studying in the evenings. Teachers are also encouraged to ride the bus and patrol the community to check up on students. Japanese teachers do not miss an opportunity to emphasize the importance of the group to their students; most of the cleaning of school property is done by the children under the supervision of the teachers. (Martial arts schools operate the same way.) This system forces students to look after school property and to ensure that their classmates do the same. In other ways, such as punishing a class of students for the behaviour of an individual, the school system teaches students to be aware of the effect of their actions and the actions of each of their classmates. Children quickly learn not to accept anybody who does not conform behaviourally, physically or mentally. Corporal punishment, bullying by teachers as well as students, and student suicides are not uncommon. Most young people have a fairly good idea of their academic standing by junior high, and those students who do not make the grade feel like failures.

To compensate for the lack of individual attention and to assist students in preparation for entrance examinations into middle school, high school and university, a private sector system of evening and afternoon cram schools, *jūku,* has developed. According to Peter Tasker in *The Japanese,* "forty per cent of Japanese children attend *jūku* at some stage; ninety per cent of those who live in metropolitan Tokyo; one hundred per cent of those who enter Japan's three most prestigious high schools." (The most prestigious high schools are those from which the largest number of students enter one of the best universities. Ten per cent of the successful candidates for Tokyo University come from three of the 5,453 high schools in Japan.) These children often spend several evenings per week studying at one of these schools; they often return home at nine or ten o'clock in the evening and continue studying. *Jūku* classes cost a great deal of money, approximately twenty per cent of the typical Japanese family budget.

Education is of overwhelming importance to Japanese parents, especially mothers, who devote their lives to their children's education. Many try to give their children a head start by enrolling them in *jūku* classes at very young ages (two and three years old) or by trying to get them into good kindergartens, which are linked to good primary and middle schools. Some of the more prestigious private universities have schools of all levels connected with them. Students who are accepted into the kindergarten have a good chance of moving relatively easily through what is referred to as the "escalator" system. As a result, these kindergartens are extremely expensive and many of them have their own entrance examinations! As Karel van Wolferen observed in *The Enigma of Japanese Power,* "Parents have been known to move to Tokyo for the sole purpose of getting their child into the right kindergarten. One maternity hospital has even advertised that delivery could be arranged as part of a package deal, guaranteeing that the baby would qualify for the right kindergarten" (p. 87). Some kindergartens have decided that it is too difficult to test three and four year olds and have opted to test the mothers instead.

High school students studying for university entrance examinations often do almost nothing but study for two years. They give up hobbies, sports, a social life and much of their sleep to focus on their studies. Whole families devote themselves to the success of their university applicant. By the time *shiken jigoku* (examination hell) rolls around in January and February, candidates and their families are in a frenzy. Failure can be devastating. Many students who fail to get into the university of their choice spend the next year attending a full-time cram school, *yobiko*, to prepare to retake the exam. For substantial fees, *yobiko* offer intensive classes designed to help students pass the examination for the university of their choice. The classes run daily from about eight o'clock until five o'clock on weekdays and often on Saturdays. Students are also expected to study at home for at least three hours each evening and all day Sunday. *Yobiko* do not have libraries or sports facilities; the focus is on absorbing the facts necessary to pass the entrance examinations.

Why do students and their parents go to these lengths? Simply put, success in the education system is the key to all that is most desirable in life: a job with a good company, prestige, contacts, enhanced attractiveness as a marriage partner (for men) and influence. Graduates of the top-ranked universities have the greatest chances of securing positions within the government bureaucracy or with one of the top businesses. And it is only the entrance process that is difficult; after acceptance, graduation is virtually assured. University life, for most students (excluding those in medicine, engineering or the physical sciences, whose careers tend to be outside the business world) is both a well-earned holiday from the unending study which characterized junior and senior high school and a break before the years of toil as a salaryman. University students spend little time studying and lots of time socializing; in Canada, the situation is reversed, with high school demanding relatively little of students, and the pressures of work and studying increasing at the university level.

The career experiences of the graduates of Japan's leading university, Tokyo University (Todai), illustrate the prizes available for the winners in the education struggle. If Japanese universities were to be placed in a pyramid according to status, Todai, and particularly its law department, would be at the very top. Karel van Wolferen described the wide-ranging opportunities for the Todai graduates in *The Enigma of Japanese Power*:

Of all the section chiefs and bureaucrats of higher rank in the Ministry of Finance, 88.6 per cent are from Todai. For the Foreign Ministry the figure is 76 per cent, for the National Land Agency 73.5 per cent and for the Ministry of Transportation 68.5 per cent. Between 80 and 90 per cent of the annual twenty to thirty recruits to the Ministry of Finance are from the Todai law department. Nearly all post-war Japanese prime ministers who exercised any influence at all have been graduates of

Todai—with the conspicuous exceptions of Tanaka Kakuei and Takeshita Noboru. In most post-war cabinets the crucial portfolios have been held by Todai graduates. Even in the cabinet of Tanaka Kakuei, seven ministers had passed through its law department. Over a quarter of all parliamentarians and more than one-third of all LDP members are Todai graduates. In the mid-1970s the number of Todai graduate executives exceeded the number of non-Todai executives in 43 of the 50 top business firms. In 1985 the presidents of 401 out of the 1,454 largest firms were Todai graduates, with another 140 and 72 from the virtually equivalent Kyoto and Hitotsubashi universities (p. 111).

Tokyo University, the University of Kyoto and the other four national universities are the most venerated universities, supplying many of the government bureaucrats and business leaders. Waseda University and Keio University in Tokyo are the two most famous and highly ranked private universities; a significant proportion of Waseda graduates become journalists or politicians, while Keio University's reputation is for producing graduates who succeed in the business world. The quality of the education received at these prestigious institutions does not determine the success of the graduates, for the instruction at Todai is often no better than that at a lower-ranked institution. What sets these universities apart is the contacts made there; most of a student's classmates are likely to end up in important positions in other ministries or companies. In addition, while large corporations and government departments searching for new recruits administer entrance exams which are theoretically open, the hiring is basically completed on a quota system, with a certain number of places reserved for graduates from the various highly ranked universities.

Rebellion and Rejection in Japan

It is perhaps not surprising to North Americans that, at different points in their lives, many young Japanese find it difficult to live within these constraints. For the majority of those who rebel, however, rebellion takes a typically Japanese form. The best illustration of such rebellion occurs in Harajuku, a district in downtown Tokyo, on Sunday afternoons. Here, young people in flamboyant clothing and often outlandish hairstyles dance, sing and perform outside for the strolling crowds. Most of the displays are group performances, and group members are usually wearing matching outfits. When afternoon turns to evening, most of these "rebels" quietly pack up their equipment, take off their wild clothing and return home to study. A more radical youth culture does exist and is well discussed in Karl Taro Greenfield's book, *Speed Tribes*. "Speed tribes" is a literal translation of the word *bosoku* and refers to the subcultures of Japanese gangsters, biker gangs, pornographic movie stars and members of ultra-right-wing movements. This is not the Japan that the government and business community displays to the world.

While most Japanese find it next to impossible to break from the group, others never have the opportunity to join. For Koreans and the *burakumin* (Japan's untouchables), entrenched patterns of discrimination prevent acceptance into mainstream Japanese society. Koreans who were born in Japan and who speak only Japanese still face difficulty in obtaining Japanese citizenship. The *burakumin*, people whose ancestors engaged in leather work or butchery, are fully Japanese and in no way physically distinguishable from mainstream citizens, and yet they continue to experience discrimination. The prejudice originates with Buddhist precepts against the taking of animal life. The *burakumin* constitute about 2 per cent of the population of Japan and live mainly in the Osaka area. Although they have had full legal equality since 1871, prejudice against them remains strong. Both of these groups go to great pains to conceal their backgrounds, but they are not usually successful. *Koseki* (family registries) give full information on family backgrounds and although it is now illegal to investigate an individual's *koseki*, prospective employers or marriage partners sometimes ask to see a copy or hire private detectives to obtain the information.

In contrast to the situation of these Koreans and the *burakumin*, the Ainu, the indigenous people of northern Japan, have had a difficult time remaining distinct. At one time, they occupied a substantial portion of the Japanese islands, but they were gradually conquered and absorbed into Japanese society. Today, fewer than 20,000 Ainu remain, only 100 of whom speak the Ainu language. Despite some recent attempts to revive the Ainu language and culture, the youngest fluent speaker of Ainu is sixty-nine years old and the outlook for revitalizing this society looks bleak.

As Japan has prospered economically, its citizens, not surprisingly, have begun to lose interest in working in the less interesting and more distasteful occupations. The Japanese refer to these as "3K" jobs: *kitsui* (severe or hard), *kitanai* (dirty) and *kiken* (dangerous).

Foreigners from the Middle East and Southeast Asia have come to Japan to find work and have taken over many of these jobs. Of the foreign workers, over 100,000 are Brazilians of Japanese ancestry, recruited for low-paid, low-status jobs. Japan is not accustomed to so many migrant workers, and there have been problems, including a tendency to blame domestic troubles on outsiders—a phenomenon which is very familiar to Canadians.

Women play a distinct and important role in Japanese society, which extends far beyond their influential contribution to their children's education. Traditional family values appear to be very strong, and women seem to live under tight restrictions, with limited expectations. However, and despite North American assumptions to the contrary, many Japanese women are quite satisfied with their lives. Content with relationships based on equality and mutual dependence and living lives that give them time to pursue their own interests, most Japanese women have not mounted a sustained challenge to the status quo. Eamonn Fingleton, a financial journalist who has reported from Tokyo for almost a decade, says in *Blindside* that "there is little evidence that Japanese women want real change. Despite five decades of Western reports of awakening feminism in Japan, Japanese women have, as mothers, perpetuated traditional sex roles in raising their children" (p. 341). For those women who do not wish to follow traditional roles, Japanese society can be stifling and limiting.

Recent changes in the lives of Japanese women are somewhat superficial and force those who want nontraditional lives to make difficult choices. A good example of both a change and its impact is the Equal Employment Opportunity Law, which went into effect in 1986. This law encourages employers to provide women with greater opportunities, and to recruit, hire and promote men and women equally. The law sought to provide highly motivated women with the opportunity to succeed. However, the bill does not outline any procedures for enforcement, and it does not provide men with corresponding equality provisions (for example, the right to choose traditional women's work). After 1986, some of Japan's larger companies (in 1989, 3 per cent of all Japanese firms and 42 per cent of Japanese companies with 5,000 employees or more) began providing two different employment tracks for their university-trained female employees. The first employment track is the traditional work: typing, filing, serving tea and providing other support functions. The Japanese call these women "office ladies" or "OLs." Most women on this track leave the company after they marry or, at the latest, after they have a child. Promotion is limited or nonexistent. The second option is the integrated track, which in theory treats women and men equally and expects women to accept transfers and work overtime as men are expected to do. Japanese companies expect a great deal from their male employees, including many hours of overtime and official socializing, frequent transfers and a firm commitment to put the company before all else. (A male Japanese worker is socialized into feeling that even phoning his wife from the office at eleven o'clock at night is a sign of weakness or disloyalty.) It is not hard to see why a marriage with both members on this career track might not succeed. To have children under these conditions, especially given the lack of child-care facilities in Japan, would be all but impossible.

Japan is a consensus-oriented society in which citizens sublimate their needs and desires to the requirements of the group, be it a family, company or nation. Given its evident rigidities and the high priority placed on achievement, it is perhaps surprising that so little rebellion surfaces. Japan has its extremists, particularly right-wing parties and the once-active Japan Red Army, and not everyone is satisfied with the existing social system, but rates of crime and violence are very low. Japanese murder rates are a small fraction of Canadian murder rates (which in turn pale in comparison with American conditions), and strict rules govern the ownership of handguns. In contrast, the Japanese enjoy almost unbridled freedom of speech, with fewer restrictions on the press and on publishers than in Canada. This situation has resulted in, for example, a proliferation of anti-Semitic literature and widespread distribution of polemical literature, much of it very extreme in nature.

Furthermore, the underworld flourishes. The *yakuza* (Japanese mafia) is comprised of roughly 100,000 gangsters. Until recently, they have remained aloof from the respectable business world. Members of the *yakuza* are usually distinguishable by their dark double-breasted suits, dark sunglasses, wide ties and permed hair. Karel van Wolferen, in *The Enigma of Japanese Power*, discusses the contention of the *yakuza* that they fulfil a social function in Japanese society:

Leaders can be interviewed about *yakuza* activities, and will argue fairly convincingly that without their organization anti-social youth would have nowhere to go and be a great nuisance. This echoes the contention of the greatest modern *yakuza* of

them all, the late Taoka Kazuo, that he made sure that the
drop-outs of society did not run wild...During a one-hour television programme devoted to the Yamaguchi-gumi [the largest
yakuza syndicate] and broadcast in August 1984 by NHK (com-
parable in function and prestige to the BBC), executives of the
mob were given the opportunity to explain their alleged great
services to society to an audience of 25 million viewers
(p. 103–104).

Although the idea of the mafia being a boon to society seems to be
absurd superficially, the argument is not without some validity. The
yakuza provide a sense of belonging to those who do not fit into
mainstream society, including members of the Korean and *burakumin* communities. The *yakuza* control their members and they follow
a code of unwritten rules: they do not sell drugs, they avoid guns,
and they endeavour to ensure that innocent bystanders are not hurt.
Not only do the *yakuza* monitor their own members, they also keep
an eye on other criminal activity and make sure that the police do
not have to deal with a large number of active individual criminals.
They do, however, manage protection rackets, run prostitution rings
and control a variety of illegal businesses, so any tendency to assign
them pure motives needs to be balanced. As long as the rules of this
arrangement are followed, the police and the *yakuza* coexisted reasonably well. Recently, though, the *yakuza* world has begun to
change: Some members have become involved in trafficking hard
drugs and in smuggling guns. Others began speculating on stocks
and property during the late 1980s and accumulated huge debts. The
yakuza have not taken well to the banks' attempts to collect, and at
least three Japanese executives have been shot in suspected *yakuza*
killings. Other high-level executives are under special police protection.

The Cycle of Japanese Life

The cycle of Japanese life runs in a much more regimented fashion
than does its Canadian counterpart. The vast majority of Japanese go
directly from high school to junior college or university, graduate at
age twenty or twenty-two and begin work immediately at a company.
Students seldom take time off to travel or to reflect on their life's
ambitions. After the drudgery of studying for university entrance
exams, four years at university are the one break most Japanese
enjoy. This is the time to let off steam, join clubs, make friends and

discover new interests. The high school years seldom allowed for relaxation, and once in a company, most *salarimen* (male, white-collar workers) are extremely busy. (OLs, although stuck in boring jobs, often have time and disposable income before they marry. This period in their lives is more relaxed.) Most Japanese join a company and stay with it for a long time, if not for life. Those Japanese who change jobs try to do so fairly early on; to be looking for a job in one's thirties indicates disloyalty or a lack of seriousness. For Japanese *salarimen*, work encompasses a good deal of their lives. They remain at work until well into the night (and often face two- to three-hour commutes, if they live in a large city), and they spend much time after work engaged in the "work socializing" that is a large part of the Japanese business world. The Japanese take few holidays (even honeymoons are quite short), since long absences from work place additional burdens on colleagues.

Not only is the pattern of life more rigid, the details and ways of doing things are also structured. The Japanese believe that correct outward form leads to proper inner behaviour and therefore that appropriate form is a vital part of Japanese life. (The expression "Excuse me" in Japanese is literally translated as "I have lost form.") The Japanese have a proper way to exchange condolences, acknowledge one's superior, celebrate the coming of the New Year, offer a drink, accept a gift and receive a compliment. A classic example of this appropriateness is the Japanese adherence to *kata,* a word that loosely translates as "the way of doing," and refers to such actions as speaking, reading, practising and so on. For instance, the formal routines associated with karate training are given the designation of *kata.* There are appropriate clothes for certain activities, appropriate foods for certain days and appropriate ages for certain events. (An old Japanese saying likens women to Christmas cake: they are no good after the twenty-fifth, as most Japanese women used to marry before age twenty-five. However, recent changes in women's approach to work have resulted in a revised version comparing Japanese women to New Year's cake, as the average marrying age has increased.) And the Japanese know the rules. Choosing a different path in life is difficult, for the social pressure to conform is pervasive and overwhelming.

Fifty years ago, Japan offered few visual signs of its contact with the West. The country had internalized Western industrial techniques and capitalized on Western knowledge, but North American popular culture had made few inroads, even with thousands of American occupation troops in Japan. Western popular culture is now ubiquitous in Japan. Musicians such as Michael Jackson and Bryan Adams are extremely popular, famous English-language actors feature prominently in bizarre television advertisements (often only on the condition that the Japanese ad not be shown anywhere else in the world), and Western fast-food chains proliferate, particularly in Tokyo. The visual transformation of Japan, which includes highways of neon lights, McDonald's and Kentucky Fried Chicken restaurants, and billboards promoting Hollywood movies, lends support to the assumption that Japan has become decisively Westernized. But this initial impression is wrong, and it leads many Western visitors to believe that Japan is, after all, not much different from North America. While the surface may appear Western, the society is, underneath, deeply Japanese.

***

For Canadians to come to terms with Japan and to better capitalize on this vital relationship, two steps are essential. First, Canada must gain a better understanding of the strengths, weaknesses and underlying assumptions that condition Canadian life. North Americans have a long-standing tradition of seeking to understand the other without first understanding themselves; this approach does not stand the country or its corporations in good stead in today's competitive world. Second, Canadians must recognize the unique qualities of Japan and Japanese society. The differences run more than skin deep, and cannot be overcome through simple translation of business and government conversations. Canadians require the assistance of cultural interpreters, as well as translators, with their introduction to Japanese life. If these two conditions are met, if Canadians reach out to Japan with a firm understanding of their own country and a willingness to learn about their Pacific partner, the relationship will have the opportunity to flourish. In contrast, if Canadians continue to insist on treating the Japanese as Asian North Americans, and criticizing rather than seeking to understand their value system, customs and social beliefs, as North Americans have done since the end of World War II, promising commercial and cultural ties will remain undeveloped.

6

Canadian and Japanese Business Cultures

On the stage of international business, Japan is truly a prominent star, while Canada remains a bit-player, little more than a background singer or a member of the dance troupe. While history and politics (particularly Canada's relationships with the United States, Britain and Japan and the country's postwar status as an important middle power) have ensured that Canada retains its place in the G-7, the assembly of the world's leading industrialized nations, it is not at all clear that the country warrants the attention and prestige associated with such membership. Japan's status, on the other hand, is unquestionable, and Western industrialized nations have encouraged Japan for years to play a more active role in international affairs.

Who could have foreseen this situation? Only fifty years ago, Japan lay in smouldering ruins, battered by American bombing attacks and psychologically bruised from the collapse of the once-impenetrable empire. Canada stood proudly alongside the victors, having contributed its share to the Allied effort (particularly in Europe); its economy was operating at full-throttle, poised to make the rapid transition from wartime military production to satisfying burgeoning postwar consumer demand. Although the United States and other Allied countries helped Japan back on its feet, while ensuring that it adopted the apparatus of liberal democracy, many observers wondered if a country so tattered and torn could rebuild and regain its place in world business affairs.

But Japan did more than rebuild; it grew and established a commercial empire that gave the country international clout far greater than that of its wartime military conquerors. And Canada, comparatively speaking, languished. The country capitalized on the general buoyancy of the postwar industrial economy, fuelled by a rip-roaring demand for mineral resources and forest products, and it discovered considerable benefits from American military involvement, first in

Korea and later in Vietnam. But the Canadian economy did not evolve in the same methodical, forward-looking way the Japanese economy did. Instead, Canada preferred to prop up aging businesses and support foundering regional economies, making decisions that rested on political rather than economic considerations. And for forty years, the country's resource wealth, massive government deficits and federal redistribution payments have papered over the inherent weaknesses of Canada's approach to economic development.

The passage of time has revealed the failings of the Canadian "plan" (if the *laissez-faire*, politically cautious approach can be so characterized) and the strength of the Japanese approach. Japan has bounced from accomplishment to accomplishment, baffling Western observers who routinely forecast the end of the Japanese miracle, and establishing new national standards for business innovation and technological adaptation. Canadians, in contrast, have maintained an enviable standard of living—one of the highest in the world—but have seen their relative economic position decline significantly over the years. The middle class in Canada has paid the price, largely in terms of extra work and ever higher expectations. At the root of these transitions are two radically different business cultures, both firmly based in national values and expectations and conditioned by the social realities of their countries. Japan's business culture works best in Japan; only certain aspects are exportable (shop-floor management techniques and the accelerated use of robotics, for example). Similarly, Canada's business culture reflects conditions within the country and is not easily transportable to a different social setting. Nevertheless, both countries can learn a great deal from the business and economic experiences of the other.

The Japanese Business Culture

Japanese business practices have, since the days of Commodore Perry, puzzled Western observers. While the nation's outlook is undoubtedly capitalistic, Japan's version is definitely capitalism with a twist. The country is competitive, aggressive and innovative, but individualism—the *sine qua non* of Western capitalism—has been kept in check. Economists have described Japan as a "capitalist development state," focusing on the strong hand that government wields in the management of the economy; but this label is incomplete. Japan's approach to business permeates the entire culture, from the education system to foreign travel, creating in the process one of the world's most dynamic economies. What, then, is this unique hybrid that has stood capitalism on its head, reinventing the Western way of doing business and beating many Western corporations at their own game?

Hundreds of books have been written about the world of Japanese business. There are books on how to do business in Japan and how to make sense of Japanese management techniques. Some extol the virtues of Japanese business, and others enumerate its flaws. A short survey can hardly do justice to the complexity of Japanese business structures, values and attitudes, but it can illustrate the fundamental differences between Japanese and Western practices. Understanding Japanese corporate culture helps not only Canadians wishing to do business with Japan but all Canadians wishing to better analyze Canada's own way of operating. Japan's notable commercial success is not an accident; it is the result of tough decisions and different approaches to management.

The difference begins at the top: stockholders do not own or control Japanese companies to any significant extent. Many companies have debt-equity ratios as high as 80:20, leaving ownership with the banks and lending companies, which supply the capital, and placing day-to-day control in the hands of company executives. Individual banks and financial institutions are backed by the Bank of Japan, behind which stands the government and the savings of the nation. (The failures of several leading financial institutions in 1995 have tested this arrangement.) The rate of personal savings in Japan is very high; the Japanese save approximately 15 per cent of their earnings, while Canadians save 10.5 per cent, Europeans save 7 per cent and Americans, 3 per cent. (Japan's high rate is partly due to the wage system whereby twice a year, in December and June, workers receive a bonus equal to a couple of months' salary. Since people are used to living on their salaries, these bonuses are often saved for major purchases.)

Because control of companies does not rest with the stockholders and therefore companies do not have to ensure high annual dividends, Japanese companies are able to focus on long-range stability and growth in market share, rather than the quarterly bottom line. The government encourages this by making tax benefits accrue to companies who reinvest their profits rather than distributing them to shareholders as dividends. This approach is of fundamental importance. Freed from both the confines of immediate profit taking and the take-over frenzy that has engulfed North American business for the past decade, Japanese firms face significantly fewer constraints on corporate initiative. They also have a clear mandate to emphasize market share, research and development, and long-term viability, elements that have proven crucial to the country's commercial success since the 1950s.

The Japanese have also eschewed the "lone wolf" approach to commerce; they do not subscribe to the belief that independence is the key to success. Instead, many Japanese businesses are linked in what are called *keiretsu* (business groups comprised of numerous companies associated with a particular manufacturer). Subsidiaries, subcontractors, suppliers and distributors form the most closely connected part of the *keiretsu*. A main bank is at the centre of the group, which also includes real estate agencies, insurance companies and trading houses. There are six enormous *keiretsu*: Mitsui, Mitsubishi, Sumitomo, Fuyo, Sanwa and Ikkan (Dai-ichi Kangyo Bank). There are also a few smaller and newer associations, which are often vertically integrated and which include a large manufacturer and all of its suppliers and distributors. The Sony group, with its eighty-seven subsidiaries and affiliated companies, is a good example of this newer form of commercial organization. Canada has a few large conglomerates, such as Power Corporation, the Pattison Group and the Irving empire, but they pale in comparison to the power and scale of the Japanese *keiretsu*.

Keiretsu members form a kind of club, looking out for each other and working to maintain business within the group. The bank plays a pivotal role by financing the operations of the member companies. Interlocking directorates tie together the nominally independent companies. From 60 to 70 per cent of company stock that is active on the Japanese stock exchange is owned by corporations, banks and other financial institutions. Through a process of "reciprocal shareholding," companies associated with a *keiretsu* hold ownership within the group, ensuring that shares are not sold but are maintained, as a means of keeping the unit strong. This stockholding system, in which *keirestu* partners hold over half of member company shares, also prevents hostile take-overs—the kind of corporate raiding that has become a North American blood sport.

The *keiretsu* is but the most obvious example of the importance of the group within Japanese business. The Japanese cultivate feelings of belonging to one large group and of working together to achieve a common goal. The amazing success of the Japanese economy since the 1950s is at least partly due to the commitment workers had to the success of their companies and to the rebuilding of Japan.

During this period of regeneration, workers blended their devotion to two groups: the company and the nation. Traditionally, Japanese workers are not likely to be lured away from their company by the prospect of better pay or perks. Companies, while demanding a great deal from their employees, also consider workers to be their greatest asset and make a long-term commitment to them. Although more Japanese are currently changing employers than was previously the case, the commitment to and from the company is much stronger than that in Canada. For Canadians, as for Americans, personal mobility and career enhancement typically take precedence over loyalty to the firm, and the individual takes priority over the group. Japanese workers are hired into a company, rather than into a specific job; it is therefore easier for them to make a lifelong commitment to the firm as career progression is more assured than it is in most Canadian companies.

This commitment to group and nation obviously influences relations between business and government. Japanese business works more closely with government than do companies in other democratic nations; the closeness of this relationship prompted some economists to suggest that Japan (and other nations such as Taiwan and South Korea) represents a third category of political economy—neither Western, nor communist. In Japan, government bureaucrats do not attempt to control business; instead, they guide the economy using information received from the business community. For instance, MITI encourages carefully selected areas of industrial activity and, as the economy changes, shifts this encouragement to more technologically advanced areas. The government has helped companies to shift their focus and move workers out of declining industries, and encouraged and organized industrywide research projects. For example, a number of Japan's top scientists from a variety of companies have been researching artificial intelligence and its applications for years, in an attempt to ensure that the country has a healthy lead in what may prove to be a pivotal economic area. (To date, the effort has met with little success.)

This tight relationship between business and government differs substantially from the Canadian model. Canadian business exercises considerable influence over government decision making, and has been a long-time beneficiary of tax breaks, government subsidies and loans, and favourable legislation. What is missing is the symbiotic relationship that exists in Japan—the idea that government should follow business and business should follow government. The Canadian focus on short-term economic considerations, company profits and political imperatives has largely prevented the country from establishing long-term objectives and priorities like those in Japan.

Generally, then, the focus of Japanese business affairs spans a much longer term. Since employees stay with companies longer, they are more concerned about the future profitability of their company. In addition, the government pays close attention to world trends and economic changes and seeks to develop current strategies to deal with these future changes. Eamonn Fingleton, a financial reporter stationed in Tokyo, argues that even major trade negotiations and disputes, such as the lengthy tussle over the importation of rice and the current round of hostile negotiations with the United States over Japanese restrictions on automobile imports, are planned and managed years ahead of time. While critics may say that Fingleton gives the Japanese too much credit for prescience, the country's commercial record over the past three decades cannot be disputed. Japanese business has been more clever, more determined and more successful in adapting to the continually changing realities of the world economy, certainly compared to resource-based, protectionist-oriented Canadian industry.

Discussions of Japanese business typically focus on the characteristics of the large corporations, without mentioning that, at the most, one-third of the Japanese work for such companies. Many of the medium and small enterprises cannot afford the benefits and structures described. A number of these smaller firms subcontract to the large manufacturing corporations, working on "just-in-time" delivery systems that leave them tremendously vulnerable to fluctuations in the market and in prices. During economic downturns, these companies, more than the large corporations, feel the pinch, in the form of lay-offs and shut-downs. In spite of the prevalence of smaller companies, the management structures of the larger corporations do set the tone for the nation and the workforce and are therefore worthy of more detailed consideration.

There is a clear rhythm to the management of Japanese companies. New employees join corporations on April 1 upon completing their education (high school for blue-collar workers and university for white-collar workers). As Japanese companies primarily hire at the entry level, all new employees are approximately the same age and have the same life experience. Few, if any, have travelled for a year, worked part-time or had any experiences that would differentiate them from their counterparts. In addition, Japanese companies prefer to hire generalists rather than specialists; they like to train in-house, so that their young employees adopt the company's philosophy and way of thinking. Very few employees have master's degrees or doctorates, although companies will sometimes send employees to the United States to earn a master of business administration after a number of years of employment. Generally speaking, graduate school is only for students seeking a career in academia.

In-house training for new employees varies from company to company, but the main purpose of the training is universal: to develop company loyalty. Some companies send their new recruits on a lengthy retreat, complete with demanding exercise regimes, corporate pep talks, and personal meditation on the meaning of becoming part of the company. Others send their new employees to a variation of army boot camp, or for Shinto training, complete with meditation sessions and cold baths. At Toyota Motor Corporation, all new male office workers spend their first seven months in training with the company. Initially, they go to Toyota City in Aichi prefecture, Toyota's headquarters and home of the company's manufacturing operations. For the first two weeks, employees learn the basic structure of a car and other technical information about Toyota's production system and corporate philosophies. Then, they work on the factory floor for three months. This "on the line" experience is designed to emphasize to employees that the most important part of Toyota is its production system and the quality of its products. This experience also ensures that future engineers and business people will have a better understanding of the jobs and lives of the factory workers. Upon completion of the factory training, the new hires work at dealerships, where they sell cars door-to-door for three months and thus learn about the retail aspects of the business. (Although door-to-door sales are declining and showroom sales are increasing, Toyota still sells a sizeable number of its cars from the door step.)

For employees at major corporations such as Toyota, this training period forms the foundation of a lifetime association with the company. The company will hold overwhelming significance throughout their lives; for some, it will even replace or supplant their personal lives. Big companies are committed to offering their employees lifetime employment. Even when the company is struggling with financial difficulties, management will go to great lengths, transferring employees from one division to another or taking cuts in pay throughout the organization, to ensure that no jobs are lost.

Companies also work hard to create a family atmosphere for their employees. Accommodation in company dormitories is available (and sometimes obligatory) for single employees, and often involves curfews (particularly for female employees) and a level of control that some people find a bit overwhelming. Subsidized housing in company subdivisions is sometimes available for married workers. Companies sponsor a variety of athletic and recreational sports teams, and English classes or classes in tea ceremony or other Japanese arts are often held in the evening. Male co-workers often go out for *otsukiai* (drinking and socializing), which builds up group morale. Company outings, such as picnics and trips to company ski resorts or to famous *onsen* (Japanese hot springs), are common. Many companies begin each work day with group callisthenics and the recitation of the company motto or the yelling of a company cheer.

No effort is spared in making employees feel loyal to the corporation and to fellow employees. Japanese managers take a much greater interest in their subordinates' lives than is the case in Canada. If a male employee is nearing thirty and is unmarried, it is common for his manager to express concern and offer to make some introductions. Managers attend weddings and graduations and offer advice and help with personal problems. If an employee gets into trouble with the law, it is the responsibility of the manager to apologize to the authorities and to the injured party on behalf of the company. (This situation exemplifies the rule that the group takes responsibility for the actions of one of its members. In one instance, the chief executive of a Japanese airline resigned after a crash involving one of the company's planes.)

Companies expect loyalty and commitment from their employees in return, and most workers have no difficulty reciprocating. A position with a large important company is prestigious, and because companies hire almost exclusively at the entry level, it is next to impossible for someone to jump from one large Japanese company to another. Large companies look for loyal employees, and a worker who is considering switching jobs is automatically seen as disloyal. Some job hopping to foreign companies does occur, but leaving a company position is not easy:

For a Japanese supervisor, losing a valued employee is a black mark. Major Japanese companies which consider employee solidarity one of their greatest strengths, put intense pressure on workers to remain loyal. Supervisors rarely can offer their people big raises in return for staying, since that would disrupt tightly controlled pay scales. So they yell at departing subordinates. They lock them in rooms and badger them. Sometimes they even appeal directly to the employees' families. Among conservative Japanese, a job-hopper may be viewed as a bit of a traitor and more than one would-be defector has stayed put because of intense family and peer pressure (*Wall Street Journal*, September 9, 1986).

The members of each year's group of new employees progress through most of their careers in step with each other in both salary and rank. The system of advancement up the company ladder, writes Arthur Whitehill in his study, *Japanese Management*, is based "upon a compromise between age-seniority and meritocracy" (p. 115). For the first ten years that an employee is with a company, individual wage or rank differentials are seldom introduced. In the subsequent years, slight differences in pay are introduced but they are minimal, and other variables (depending on family situation and type of work) are built into the system: hence, it becomes difficult for an employee to make a direct comparison with others. The first promotion to section head occurs after a person has been with a company between ten and fifteen years. It is only around this time that employees would begin to discover differences in the number of years before promotion among employees or to realize which employees attained the more desirable positions and thereby gain some understanding of their status in the promotion race.

Because the rank differentials are so small, employees continue to feel they are candidates for promotion and to work hard for a long time. They see themselves as members of a team and work for its benefit. Even the poorest of employees will eventually reach the level of *kakaricho* (loosely translated as chief clerk or section head), and most become *kacho* (manager or section head), the next rung up the ladder, at some point. It is only nearer the top of the hierarchy that the more able employees are selected for the director and chief executive positions and the remainder retire or receive positions in affiliated companies. An employee is not normally asked to report to a superior who is of the same age group or who is younger. This arrangement enables supervisors to promote the work of subordinates without fearing that the younger employees may take their jobs. Naturally, within this system of lifetime employment, there are always people who are incompetent or who do not pull their weight.

They are referred to as *madogiwazoku* (window-seat tribe) and are given desks but no work or responsibilities. While they may be a liability to the company, the benefit of demonstrating the commitment to lifelong security outweighs the cost of keeping a less-productive employee on staff. (Other people are passed over for promotion simply because there are too many people in their age group for the number of available positions.)

Lifetime employment and the seniority-based promotion and pay system depend on a rapidly growing economy. These practices become much harder to maintain when the economy is slowing down or stagnating; the company's employee profile quickly becomes top-heavy, necessitating the elimination of many people at the top and middle ranks. As well, the country's remarkable commitment to the introduction of robots in factories has displaced workers and raised concerns about companies' ability to maintain high levels of employment. However, automation allows Japan to adapt to the fact that, over time, fewer people will be entering the workforce as a consequence of declining birth rates.

Traditionally, the mandatory retirement age in Japan has ranged from fifty-five to fifty-seven, although changing demographics have forced the government to raise it to sixty. Many corporations, however, are actually retiring younger and younger workers. It is now not unheard of for *salarimen* as young as forty-five to be retired. However, financial considerations dictate that for very few of these people does retirement actually mean the end of work, particularly since companies are not required to set up pension plans; instead, employees usually receive a single lump-sum separation payment. For those who have worked their entire career for a large Japanese company, the lump-sum separation payment may be sufficiently large to enable the retiree to start up a small business. In contrast, retirees from smaller or less prosperous companies may not receive enough money to live on and may be forced to seek other work. Some companies keep on some of these retired employees as "temporary workers" at reduced wages and benefits.

Employees usually move from one division to another every four or five years. This rotation allows people to gain experience in many different parts of the company; by the time employees reach the level of general manager, they are familiar with all aspects of the company. Critics say that people in this system have no particular areas of expertise, while proponents argue that this lack of specialization is more than offset by the employee's broader understanding of the corporation. Specific job descriptions are exceedingly rare in Japan. Unlike Western corporations, where detailed job descriptions and contracts outlining specific duties are the norm, Japanese companies simply assume that their employees will do what needs doing.

In general, accountability, authority and duties are the three parameters that give definition to a job. According to Japan specialist John Shook:

These three factors are given markedly differing weights in a Japanese versus a Western company. And this difference translates into a significant contrast in the individual's sense of his or her own personal role within the organization...[In Japan,] accountability (responsibility) is the only one of the three parameters with any real meaning at all. More than a simple reversal in order (from duties to authority to accountability), duties and authority are incidentals that are decided fully by the scope of one's accountability. Questions of duties and authority never come up outside of the context of recognizing boundaries of accountability (John Shook, unpublished memorandum on Japanese management).

Japanese employees, therefore, feel accountable for the activities of their department and even their companies to a much greater extent than do their Western counterparts. They even feel accountable and can, to a certain extent, be held responsible for, events or circumstances over which they had no direct control. Japanese employees rarely give excuses or explanations to their supervisors for tardiness or errors or incomplete work. They simply apologize. The weight of this responsibility is very keenly felt, and it breeds in Japanese employees a desire to both avoid making decisions and to check and confirm decisions with superiors. For this reason, *kakunin denwa* (confirmation phone calls) are very common. A staff member planning a meeting between his manager and someone from another company will phone the person from the other company many times to ensure that that person has not forgotten the meeting. If the guest does not show up and the manager is kept waiting, it is the staff member's fault, so every effort is made to ensure that the guest arrives.

Japanese offices are very open; they lack the structure and separation that is typical in a North American office setting. Only the most senior people have their own offices; all other desks are set up in the middle of a large room. The desks sit in long rows facing each other, to better enable workers to consult with one another (and socialize). At the end, facing the rows perpendicularly, is the manager's desk. A small distance behind this desk is the general manager's desk. A typical department would consist of two or three sections (*ka*), about fifty regular workers, a manager for each section and one or two general managers. There are often two or three departments on a single office floor. Of the fifty employees in a department, about twenty are Office Ladies—women who do the word processing, make copies, serve tea and assist in the general office operations. Within the group of regular employees, there is a hierarchy based on the number of years a person has been with the company. All employees are aware of who joined the company when, and everyone, from all departments, who entered the company in the same year is referred to as being in the same *dōki*.

Within Japanese companies, there are some staggering differences between the efficiencies of the factory and the inefficiencies of the office. Corporations such as Toyota and Honda are famous for their use of the just-in-time delivery system. Rather than maintaining large inventories of parts, the manufacturers take delivery of material from subcontractors according to a tight, rigid schedule. In this fashion, large corporations transfer the responsibility for maintaining inventory to smaller companies, and are thus able to expand or contract their production with relative ease. The use of this system, together with other productivity improvements (robots, extremely efficient floor management techniques and advanced transportation systems), has made Japanese corporations world leaders in efficient, cost-effective manufacturing.

One of Japan's most important innovations, and certainly one that has been widely copied outside of Japan, has been the introduction of Quality Control Circles (QCC). Work teams and supervisors meet regularly to police the quality of work they produce and to seek ways to do their jobs better. Work teams compete against each other to try and produce more suggestions for eliminating waste in any form (wasted motion, wasted time), for decreasing the rate of defects and for saving money. There are often prizes for teams or individuals who come up with particularly good suggestions. Companies compete for the Deming Prize (named after W. Edwards Deming, the American who invented many of the management techniques that Japan embraced but whose advice was ignored for years in his home country), which recognizes "outstanding achievement in productivity and quality control."

Japanese workers bend over backwards to come up with suggestions that will benefit their companies. According to Jared Taylor, author of *Shadows of the Rising Sun*:

In 1981, the Toyota Motor Company's 48,000 employees came up with 1.3 million formal suggestions to improve quality or lower costs. That was 27 suggestions per employee! *Ninety per cent* were accepted by management for an estimated savings that year of $45 million. At the Zama factory of Toyota's competitor, the Nissan Motor Corporation, there were only 17 suggestions per employee in 1979. The factory manager thinks that's not bad. After all, he points out, the Zama factory is already the most highly automated car assembly plant in the world and is already so efficient that there are no more improvements a single employee is likely to think of. His men got together in groups after work to think up their 17 suggestions each (p. 171–172).

Office management is not as tightly or efficiently organized. Unlike the North American top-to-bottom, decision-making model, the Japanese style is said to be "bottom-up". In truth, notes John Shook, "Bottom-up management refers not so much to 'decision making' as to proposal generating. Front-line employees, those closest to the action, are expected to continually generate ideas." Co-workers and supervisors discuss these ideas and develop proposals, which pass through the formal authorization process. Authorization involves sending the documents first to the assistant manager and the manager for approval. If one of them requests alterations, the employee makes those changes and sends it back to the manager. The manager, upon approving the document, sends it up to the general manager. The document continues up and down the ladder until it has reached the ultimate destination, a director, the chair or the president, depending on the document's importance. The director accepts or rejects the document, or sends it back for more revisions. Members of the department affix their personal seal (*hanko*) on the document to indicate approval. This method of circulating documents, referred to as *ringi seido*, is a long and time-consuming process, but it guarantees that once a proposal has been officially approved, all members of the department concerned have been fully briefed and are on side. (To emphasize how much time these decisions take, a Japan Economic Survey discovered that 70 per cent to 80 per cent of managerial staff participate in decision making.)

Along the same lines, there is extensive behind-the-scenes consultation with all affected parties before a new project is undertaken. The Japanese refer to this as *nemawashi*, which means cutting around the roots of a tree before transplanting it (as opposed to someone on high making a decision and yanking out the tree by its trunk). The practice of *nemawashi* is designed to minimize conflicts and build consensus. By the time an actual meeting is scheduled to take place, all parties have been consulted and the promoter of the project has a strong sense of whether or not the majority of employees support it.

The Japanese place a very high priority on planning. They have a strong desire to understand every angle of a situation, and they ask questions about the tiniest of details. In his book *How to Do Business with the Japanese*, Mark Zimmerman attributes part of this great attention to detail to the Japanese education system:

But one major consequence of the system that a business person must be aware of is that the study habits a Japanese salary man began acquiring when he was five make him a compulsive doer of homework. No detail is too small for him to go over; no bit of information is considered irrelevant when studying a problem. He regards absolutely nothing as too much trouble. This capacity for study means that if you are dealing with a Japanese businessman, you can be sure that his preparation for the meeting will always be five steps ahead of yours. They have no concept of the favorite American pastime of "winging it." From preparing for business meetings to preparing to enter a foreign market, the Japanese executive's capacity for sheer doggedness is immense. This is perhaps one of the main reasons why the Japanese know so much more about us and our markets than we do about them (p.19).

This emphasis on planning and negotiating ensures that the project is well considered and in line with other company activities and goals. Unfortunately, many Western companies become frustrated with the time it takes for a Japanese company to reach a decision. (Mark Zimmerman highlights the Japanese love of technical detail and desire to have each item in a document discussed and analyzed at length. As a humourous aside, he mentions the way waiters in French restaurants in Japan must "read, translate, and explain each and every item on the menu, including a short dissertation on the natural history of any unusual ingredients" [p.32].) Once a Japanese company has reached a decision, however, it is ready to move immediately. By this time, the company has consulted all parties, finalized all details, and is firmly committed to the project. Western companies often work in the opposite fashion, making a quick agreement based on corporate or individual intuition, and then consulting with staff and examining the project details.

Because Japanese management emphasizes planning, especially for the long term, it is often fairly unconcerned about short-term waste of time, energy and talent. Patience is drilled into the Japanese office worker. New employees often spend the first year with very little to do; they are supposed to slowly absorb the company philosophy and learn through observation. A Western company would see an idle employee as an unnecessary expense, and the employee would probably be bored and discontented. Japanese management, however, knows that it will make good use of this employee in the future, so it is not concerned. Over the years, patience is reinforced by the continual planning, revising and renegotiating that is required of employees. They become accustomed to this process and do not get discouraged if asked to make seemingly endless revisions of a project. While employees who will rework a project until it is deemed acceptable are an asset, this kind of inculcated patience also brings disadvantges. Youthful enthusiasm and a burning desire to create, invent, participate and change are quickly hammered out of individuals who are forced to wait quietly and patiently.

Not surprisingly, elements of Japanese management practice carry over into the operation of labour organizations. Although more standard trade unions remain in some sectors, since the 1960s, most major Japanese corporations have had enterprise unions, which represent the employees in one company rather than those in an entire industry. This type of union developed in response to a series of major strikes that convinced the government and the corporations that industry-wide unionism hampered company and national progress. The enterprise unions brought more peaceful company-worker relationships, but at the cost of worker freedom. Naturally, if one union strikes and its company's production stops, other companies in the same industry can snatch up the customers of the company on strike. Since the union would also lose under these circumstances, strikes of any duration are exceedingly rare. In larger private companies, then, unions and management work closely together to achieve the long-term goals of the company. Strikes, such as they are (they can be as short as one day or even fifteen minutes!), are used simply to notify management that the union is upset and serious. Every March, union federations and employers' associations negotiate base-rate salary increases for all employees. These groups agree on a guideline of a given percentage increase; each company must come as close to the guideline as possible. This annual event is called the Shunto or Spring Labour Offensive, and it provides a comparatively conflict-free means of reaching wage settlements. The relative harmony between management and the union, of course, creates problems for those workers who have a serious grievance with the company.

The Canadian approach to labour-management relations, highlighted by confrontation, lengthy strikes, grievance committees and internal company tensions, stands in sharp contrast to the Japanese model. While contemporary anti-union sentiment has heightened criticism of the union-shop concept, this arrangement has actually served Canadian business and workers quite well. Canadian industrial plants are highly efficient, have generally adapted well to technological innovation and capitalized on the advanced skills and education of Canadian workers. At the same time, however, recent lay-offs and pay reductions have eroded worker loyalty to companies, and enhanced the adversarial nature of labour-management relations.

The Japanese corporation and Japanese business in general are far from perfect. While there have been efforts to emulate and attempts to ridicule Japanese business practices, the simple truth is that this approach works well in Japan because it is rooted in Japanese culture. Respect for the group (in this case, the company), long-term outlook and willingness to sublimate individual gain to collective achievement are deeply imbedded in Japanese society. None of these elements are integral to North American society. While Canadian business can learn a great deal from the Japanese about industrial technology, shop-floor management and the value of research and development, Canadian firms can no more escape the confines of Canadian culture than Japanese corporations can ignore Japanese values. As the economic results of the last three decades reveal, however, Japan's approach to business and business management is uniquely well suited to the combination of globalized trade, technological innovation, the need for research and development, and the importance of corporate-government interaction.

Canadian and Japanese Business Cultures Compared

The degree to which business values and assumptions actually differ in Japan and Canada remains to be seen. While it is relatively easy to point to contrasts in Canadian and Japanese business practices and managerial techniques, it is harder to ascertain the fundamental dissonance between the two countries' corporate and management value systems. In a recent book, *The Seven Cultures of Capitalism*, Charles Hampden-Turner and Alfons Trompenaars provide a window on the different national corporate value systems. The authors surveyed hundreds of business executives in different countries, asking a variety of questions and presenting numerous scenarios of decision making to ascertain the distinctions between countries. (The seven cultures explored are the United States, Japan, Germany, France, Britain, Sweden and the Netherlands, although the surveys covered many other countries as well.) The study revealed stark differences in values, assumptions and priorities, which help explain the current direction (and potential fate) of the national economies. An examination of a few of the cases detailed in *Seven Cultures* illustrates two points: the striking similarities between Canada and the United States, and the marked differences between the business cultures of North America and Japan. Canada and Japan differed substantially on key issues: the importance of corporate profit, which many Canadian managers saw as the sole goal for the company; the role of individual achievement, which was twice as important to Canadians as to the Japanese; loyalty to the firm, which showed the reverse trend; and the source of managers' power, which Canadians saw as skill, and the Japanese saw as rank. On the crucial issue of business leaders' willingness to adopt a long-term view of corporate matters, Japan topped the list; Canada tied with Thailand for fourteenth and the United States was nineteenth.

Seven Cultures examines dozens of variables (of which the above summary represents only a small sample). On some issues, there were greater differences between Canadians and Americans and more similarities between North American and Japanese business. But this trend is not representative of the general situation. Canadian business culture is little more than a northern extension of the American way of doing business—although Canadian managers are ranked lower for "drive and responsibility" (likely a reflection of the country's branch plant ethos, which removes a substantial degree of managerial autonomy from Canadian companies and leaves major decision-making authority in the hands of foreign-based executives). The symmetry between Canadian and American business cultures explains the remarkable ease with which business is conducted across the Canada–United States boundary; the dissonance between North American and Japanese business values, attitudes and assumptions helps explain the considerable difficulty North Americans experience in creating and maintaining effective business contacts across the Pacific.

Seven Cultures provides an interesting summary of the differences between the North American and Japanese approaches to business. In the United States, the old adage "time is money" takes precedence; in Japan, time is perceived as an ally, providing an opportunity to accumulate knowledge, which is seen as more important than short-term profits. Americans (and Canadians) define their organization as a "machine." The Japanese see their companies as an "organism" and take a wholistic view. North Americans, working in a highly competitive marketplace, see their professional careers as a race up—and down—a staircase, with individual merit determining one's success. The Japanese (and, interestingly, the Spanish and Singaporeans) view their careers as being analogous to a roller-coaster ride, influenced by uncontrollable forces to which they must adapt. This is not to say that one system is an improvement on the other, for all approaches have their strengths and weaknesses. However, this study provides an excellent illustration of a vital point: Canadians and the Japanese approach the "business of business" in radically different fashions, reflecting the social, philosophical, historical and intellectual cultures from which they emerged.

***

The next decade holds great promise and uncertainty for Canadian and Japanese business. In both countries, complex, interrelated developments in finance, government and commerce have changed the essential nature of the commercial world. In Canada, the business community has long lobbied for provincial and federal governments to take a more businesslike approach to its affairs, and its wishes have finally been heeded. Japan faces different pressures, including increasing protectionism of its trading partners and the continued high value of the yen.

At one level, these pressures are nothing new, for both Canada and Japan have undergone massive business transformations over the past thirty years. Japan has responded more creatively and effectively to a changing world, while Canadian business has adapted much more slowly to new realities. What is clear is that a substantial gap in business practices, outlook and management style remains between Canada and Japan. The coming decades will reveal which approach is best suited for the fast-moving, technologically sophisticated and globalized trading environment of the twenty-first century. On the basis of the past thirty years, Canadians have good reason to be concerned about the ability of their business culture to capitalize on opportunities and avoid pitfalls in the rapidly changing commercial world; the Japanese, in contrast, can anticipate with considerable confidence that the skills, models and approaches that enabled them to adapt to postwar economic conditions will stand the country in good stead as it confronts the new commercial conditions. Only time, of course, will tell.

7

The Evolution of Canada-Japan Trade

Japan stands at the forefront of trading nations, having built a dynamic, outward-looking and innovative economy tied to the rapidly changing needs of the industrial world. Japan's trade is so extensive that the ubiquitous Japanese automobile now dominates the world's markets, the country's electronic firms have outlets around the world and high-technology Japanese manufacturers dominate industrial trade. In contrast, Canada relies heavily on the exporting of its natural resources and manufactured products and imports vast quantities of material each year. Canada's trade accomplishments have been much more modest, restricted to wheat, forest products and minerals, and have not changed significantly over the years, despite the remarkable dynamism of modern global markets.

Japan's trading patterns and marked success have generated tremendous controversy. The current massive Japanese surplus—Japan exported over $350 billion and imported $236 billion in 1993—provokes endless discussion and considerable resentment from principal trading partners and leads to countless demands for Japan to relax import regulations and purchase more foreign goods. In the same year, the United States exported $465 billion worth of goods and imported $603 billion, resulting in a massive trade deficit of almost $140 billion (over $40 billion of this deficit was with Japan). Canada exported $177 billion and imported $169 billion in 1993, leaving a small trade surplus of $7.3 billion.

The imbalance of Japan's trade with the United States is the basis of the current debate about the extraordinary value of the Japanese yen, the insistence that Japan open its markets to more imported goods, and the possibility of American trade retaliation against Japan for its failure to comply to U.S. satisfaction. The threat of retaliation will grow if the Japanese do not make changes in the automotive sector. Canada also faces severe imbalances in its trade relations with

Japan, masking the otherwise rosy picture presented by national data, and it lacks the international clout to make its trading situation of broader significance. In 1993, for example, Canada rang up a resounding $28.8-billion trade surplus with the United States, an artifact of the Canada–United States Free Trade Agreement, the vibrant American economy and, in particular, the success of the Canadian automobile industry. In contrast, Canada's imports from Japan totalled $2.3 billion more than the country's exports to Japan; contrary to popular perception, Canada has been in a trade deficit position with Japan since 1984.

This tale of two trading countries—one, the world's most creative and wide-reaching, and the other, tied to the umbilical cord of American prosperity—illustrates the profoundly different paths that Japan and Canada have taken in the postwar world. Japan has a relatively balanced trading network, sending 34 per cent of its exports to the United States, 22 per cent to Southeast Asia, 21 per cent to Western Europe and 5 per cent to the Middle East. Canada, in contrast, sends about 80 per cent of its exports to the United States, less than 5 per cent to Japan and only 1.6 per cent to the United Kingdom, its third-largest trading partner. The rhetoric of Canadian trade, a hallmark of national politics since the last century has substantially remained as rhetoric. Canada's economy is remarkably dependent, its economic future linked to the seemingly essential but potentially unreliable American engine. Meanwhile, connections with the more dynamic, innovative and faster-growing Japanese market have been substantially ignored.

The Canada-Japan trading relationship is far from new, for its roots stretch back over 120 years and it has emerged as Canada's second most important trading connection. Canada, in contrast, is of considerably less importance to Japan and accounts for only 4.8 per cent of Japan's total trade. Canada was recently ranked as Japan's fifteenth largest export destination, while it was the 6th largest importer into Japan. The evolution of this relationship reveals a great deal about the manner in which both countries approach international trade; it illustrates Japan's notable success in penetrating Canadian markets and indicates the minor accomplishments of Canadian business in finding a non-resource niche within the Japanese economy.

A Brief History of Canada-Japan Trade

Trade between Canada and Japan began long before the establishment of diplomatic relations between the two countries. The first indications of trade appeared in the late 1870s; ironically, given Canada's resource-dominated trade with Japan, the first shipment sent from Canada to Japan consisted of manufactured goods. In the mid-1880s, with the completion of the transcontinental railway and the establishment of shipping connections between the two countries, regular trade began to grow steadily.

Canada sought markets for its traditional trading products, primarily forest products, grain and fish, hoping to offset declining trade with Britain and avoid too great a dependence on the United States. Canada exported lumber and wooden ships' masts to Japan in 1886 and a small amount of coal in 1891. The first shipments of wheat and salted herring were exported in 1892, followed by salted salmon in 1896 and Douglas fir lumber in 1903. Japanese immigrants in Canada were among the first to identify the potential trade opportunities across the Pacific, and these small traders led the way in establishing business connections with Japan.

Japan entered the international market place with tea and silk. The initial shipment of silk from Japan reached Canada in 1887. Silk was to Japan what wheat was to Canada in the late nineteenth century, earning 40 per cent of Japan's foreign exchange. Silk and tea comprised Japan's crucial resources and enabled the country to purchase foreign technology and manufactured goods. Japan's rapid industrialization rested, ironically, on the exporting of this most traditional Japanese product. By the late 1920s, silk represented over 60 per cent of Canada's imports from Japan. "Silk Expresses," Canadian Pacific trains transporting the raw product to textile mills in New York where it was used mostly for women's stockings, burst into prominence.

Over the years, Canada found ready markets in Japan for its raw materials, but this seldom resulted from Canadian initiative. Early in the century, the Japanese consul general in Canada, Tatsugoro Nosse, observed that Japanese buyers had difficulty finding Canadian firms interested in selling to the Japanese market. Instead, large Japanese trading companies actively sought out Canadian products, particularly raw materials, often guaranteeing or financing part of the cost of extracting the resources. In traditional Canadian fashion, Canadian business devoted more energy to restricting imports, in textiles and electronics for example, than to promoting its exports to interested countries such as Japan.

Wilfrid Laurier, prime minister from 1896 to 1911, was the first Canadian leader to become truly enthusiastic about the prospects for

Canadian trade with Japan. Laurier and his ministers believed Canada could export pulp and paper, fresh and canned fruit, preserved beef, pork, butter, cheese and fish to this newly found market. Their most hearty enthusiasm was reserved for the export potential of wheat, because the prime minister felt that bread could replace rice as the staple food of Japan. The Japanese failed to fit into Laurier's grand scheme, but the prime minister's vision of transcontinental prosperity ensured that the Canadian government began to take Japan seriously.

By the time diplomatic relations were established between the two countries in 1929, Japan had become Canada's fifth-largest trading partner, with 3.1 per cent of Canada's exports going to Japan and 1.0 per cent of Canada's imports coming from Japan. (Canada sent 36.7 per cent of its exports to the United States and 31.5 per cent to the United Kingdom that same year.) Canada's exports consisted mostly of wheat and flour (51 per cent of total exports to Japan), fish, and wood products. Japan's rapid industrial expansion during World War I created additional opportunities: Canada began to export lead, nickel, zinc and aluminum on a relatively large scale, and Japan became a principal customer for these products.

In the pre–World War II period, when Canada was either slightly ahead of or on par with Japan in industrial terms, markets also existed for Canadian manufactured products. A few items, including shoes, tires, automobiles and electrical equipment, found Japanese purchasers, and in 1935, manufactured goods represented 24.5 per cent of Canadian exports to Japan, although the reduction of resource exports caused by trade conflicts between the two nations was an influential factor. The problem began in 1931 when Canada increased tariffs on certain goods coming into Canada; these duties fell disproportionately on Japanese imports. In retaliation, the Japanese government soon placed an additional 50 per cent duty on Canadian wheat, flour, lumber, wood pulp and wrapping paper. Canada responded in kind, levying a 33.3 per cent duty on all Japanese imports. The 1935 Canadian election resulted in a change of government and the introduction of a less protectionist trade policy. The new regulations saw a return to preexisting trade arrangements, with manufactured products dropping to less than 2 per cent of total Canadian exports.

Generally, Japan did not figure prominently in Canadian import markets, which remained the domain of American and British traders, and even the small flow of Japanese goods began to dry up in

Table 1
Canada's Trade with Japan,
Selected Years, 1886 – 1940
(In $ millions)

Year	Exports	Imports
1886	2	1,486
1888	56	1,554
1890	27	1,259
1895	10	1,573
1900	112	1,763
1905	509	1,929
1910	659	2,180
1915	964	2,783
1920	7,733	13,637
1922	14,832	8,195
1925	22,046	6,985
1929	42,100	12,921
1930	30,476	12,537
1935	16,936	4,425
1940	26,000	4,055

Source: Statistics Canada. Various reports on Canada's International Trade.

the 1930s. As cotton and manufactured textiles (such as rayon) replaced silk, the traditional Japanese trade evaporated. Canadian businesses imported a small volume of household and novelty goods, but Japan actually offered little that Canada could not buy more cheaply or more reliably elsewhere.

Trade between Canada and Japan levelled off at the end of the World War I (see Table 1), but three years later, in 1922, Canadian exports to Japan surpassed Japanese exports to Canada for the first time. Japanese exports languished through the 1920s and 1930s, while Canadian sales to Japan grew substantially. In 1929, Canadian

Table 2
Canada's Trade with Japan
Selected Years, 1946 – 1956
(in $ millions)

Year	Exports	Imports
1946	1,024	3
1948	8,001	3,144
1950	20,533	12,087
1952	102,603	13,162
1954	96,474	19,197
1956	127,870	60,826

Source: Statistics Canada. Various Reports on Canada's International Trade.

exports hit a prewar high of over $42 million, almost $30 million more than Japan managed to sell to Canada that same year.

Japan's aggressive tactics in the Far East in the 1930s slowed prewar commercial relations considerably. Canadians reacted to Japanese expansionism and military prowess by introducing a series of trade restrictions, only to have Japan retaliate in kind. When war broke out in 1941, trade screeched to a halt and did not resume for the duration of the conflict. Only in 1947, with the Allied occupation fully in place in Japan and most of the wartime leadership relegated to the sidelines, did Canada reestablish trade contacts with Japan. Lingering wartime stereotypes and hostilities in conjunction with the devastation wrought on Japan's economy prevented rapid expansion of commercial links.

Japan was physically and psychologically flattened by the final stages of the war. Defeated by the final American bombardments, Japan now faced the formidable task of rebuilding. The country desperately needed food and the raw materials necessary to revive its crippled industries. Traditional Asian suppliers, themselves recovering from the war or, as in China, engulfed in revolution, could not readily meet Japan's needs; but Canada could. It had abundant grain, forest products and minerals, and a sizeable industrial base, which was hastily being retooled from the production of military materials to the manufacturing of consumer goods. Japanese authorities were soon worried about an overdependence on Canadian resources, particularly since Canada was reluctant to purchase Japanese goods. Anxious to continue selling to a rapidly rebuilding Japan, Canadian politicians and business leaders recognized Japanese concerns and began to open the Canadian market to Japanese imports, principally inexpensive manufactured goods, textiles and clothing.

Canadian consumers benefited from the importation of cheap Japanese trade goods, which capitalized on abundant, inexpensive Japanese labour. The Japanese turned to the revitalization of their economy with the same determination they had committed to the war effort, and by the mid-1950s, cheap imports from Japan flooded into Western markets. Competing Canadian industries, particularly a beleaguered domestic textile industry long-sustained by protective tariffs and government benevolence, suffered serious losses. But Canadian appetites had been whetted by cheap Japanese imports, and there was little prospect of closing off these trade ties. Canadians could scarcely complain: exports to Japan topped $125 million in 1956, a figure more than three times higher than that of the best pre–World War II annual trade, and even though imports sky-rocketed from slightly more than $3 million in 1948 to over $60 million by 1956, Canada maintained a very favourable balance of trade with Japan (see Table 2).

Canada-Japan Trade, 1950s to 1985

Over the next thirty years, until the dramatic reorientation of Japanese trade in the mid-1980s, Canada-Japan trade followed the basic track laid down in the postwar period. Canada sold an ever increasing volume of raw materials to Japan, including minerals, lumber, pulp and paper and foodstuffs, and purchased an equally rapidly growing quantity of manufactured goods from the Japanese. Canada maintained a healthy surplus throughout this period (except in 1972 when imports from Japan exceeded Canadian exports); this surplus reinforced Canada's continued belief that the seemingly inexhaustible supply of resources would sustain prosperity indefinitely (see Table 3).

The principal change in this period occurred on the Japanese side. Through the 1960s, Japan's exports to Canada consisted of low-priced, inexpensively produced consumer goods that gave the label "made in Japan" an unappealing public image. Canadian competitors, particularly in the textile trades, maintained their criticism of

Table 3
Canada's Trade with Japan
Selected Years, 1958 – 1984
(in $ millions)

Year	Exports	Imports
1958	105.0	70.2
1960	178.8	110.0
1962	214.5	125.3
1964	330.2	174.3
1966	393.8	253.0
1968	606.1	360.0
1970	810.1	581.7
1972	964.7	1,017.0
1974	2,219.7	1,423.0
1976	2,388.0	1,525.6
1978	3,051.2	2,268.4
1980	4,370.5	2,792.1
1982	4,568.4	3,526.8
1983	4,721.7	4,412.9
1984*	5,640.8	5,710.8

* This year marks the shift from a surplus to a deficit in Canada's trade with Japan.

Source: Statistics Canada. Various reports on Canada's International Trade.

"unfair" Japanese trade, but it was limited consumer interest that placed a cap on the value and impact of Japanese trade goods. Soon though, Japan began the reorientation of its economy that became the country's hallmark. It handed over the manufacturing of low-end products to the new low-wage economies in Southeast Asia and reoriented its industrial plant to focus on new technologies, particularly steel, automobile manufacturing and shipbuilding.

The first automobiles matched the Japanese reputation for "cheap" goods. The early Datsun (Nissan), Toyota and Honda products were inexpensive, lightly built and small, and they were quickly adopted as commuter vehicles and second family cars. North American manufacturers paid little attention, scarcely perceiving the Japanese cars as a threat, so confident were they of their hold on market share. They were wrong, although consumer loyalty to the Big Three North American automobile manufacturers (Chrysler, Ford and General Motors) has proved reasonably strong. The quality of Japanese products improved dramatically from the 1960s to the mid-1970s, with automobiles moving from low-end consumer vehicles to high-quality, reasonably priced, and eminently reliable midrange vehicles. Cars such as the Honda Civic, Toyota Corolla and Datsun 610 became familiar on Canadian roads, and the more expensive Datsun 240Z, Mazda RX7 and four-wheel-drive vehicles competed favourably with North American products.

Japan quickly capitalized on other commercial opportunities. Although the Japanese, at this point, developed few new products on their own, they perfected the art of copying and adapting expensive items for mass consumption. Miniaturization and the use of transistors sparked a veritable flood of Japanese electronics into North America, pushing many North American companies out of the market. Japanese manufacturers and traders had completed a stunning reversal of corporate and national imagery, establishing Japanese products at the forefront of the consumer electronics revolution.

Canada-Japan Trade after the Plaza Accord

Japan's trading arrangements changed dramatically after the Plaza Accord of 1985. In the early 1980s, the overvalued American dollar and undervalued Japanese yen had created a trade surplus for Japan that became unacceptable for its trading partners. The 1985 Plaza Accord, negotiated by the finance ministers of the key industrialized nations, sought to correct the situation by realigning the exchange rates. In 1985–86, the Japanese yen virtually doubled in value, and Japan's international competitiveness was dramatically affected. Over the next few years, Japan's economy went through a number of changes in an attempt to cope. The country moved labour-intensive manufacturing offshore, stimulated domestic consumer demand and invested in high-technology industries. All of these developments had a decisive impact on the country's trading relationships. Japan's trading partners had anticipated that the revaluation of the yen would cause disruptions in the Japanese economy and permit them to regain lost market share. Not for the first or last time, these countries underestimated Japan's resourcefulness and its willingness to change and respond to new economic circumstances. What initially appeared to be a bitter pill for the Japanese soon took on the characteristics of a magic elixir. Although many export prices did increase due to the reevaluation, such increases are expected for exporting countries facing a rise in the value of their currency. Japanese companies were unusually quick to note the effects and reorient their trading and manufacturing operations accordingly.

Japan responded quickly to the new realities. Resource products, which in 1985 comprised two-thirds of Japanese imports, represented only 50 per cent by 1991. Japanese non-oil imports rose from a value of slightly less than $100 billion (U.S.) to $200 billion (U.S.) in the six years following the Plaza Accord. The rate of growth for imported manufactured goods, in particular, sky-rocketed. Between 1985 and 1991, imports of machinery and equipment rose 246.4 per cent, helping to break the traditional Japanese pattern of importing raw materials and exporting finished products.

Canada participated only marginally in the great import explosion in Japan. (See Tables 4 and 5.) While total Japanese non-oil imports grew by 124 per cent from 1985 to 1991, imports from Canada increased by only 60.1 per cent. According to a study by the Canadian Embassy in Tokyo, Canada actually experienced a decline in its share of Japan's non-oil imports, from 5.4 per cent in 1985 to 3.9 per cent in 1991. The cost to Canada of failing to simply hold on to its share of the Japanese trade was a loss of $3.5 billion in exports in 1992. This decline can be traced to two factors: First, Japan's import profile had shifted rapidly while Canada's emphasis had remained on the exporting of raw and semiprocessed materials. Second, not only are Canada's top ten exports to Japan resource products, but eight of these experienced sales declines in this period. Canada faced more competition than ever in the resource export business, and it did not fare as well in the Japanese market as competitors such as New Zealand (in raw logs and timber, fish and shellfish), Australia (in coal and meat) and the United States (in fish and seafood, meat and fruits and vegetables).

These losses aside, there were a handful of promising developments. Japanese imports of machinery and equipment from Canada rose 232.8 per cent in this period, and grew to 4 per cent of total Japanese imports from Canada. While these are impressive increases,

Table 4 Canada's Trade with Japan 1986 – 1994 (in Cdn. $ millions)		
Year	Exports	Imports
1986	5,941,999	7,632,155
1987	7,036,247	7,550,709
1988	8,708,490	9,267,633
1989	8,797,262	9,563,089
1990	8,186,387	9,525,226
1991	7,119,416	10,262,068
1992	7,452,222	10,762,191
1993	8,430,100	10,722,500
1994	9,547,500	11,343,300
Source: *Canada-Japan Trade Council Newsletter* (March–April 1995).		

they did not offset the decline in the resource sector. Overdependence on the resource sector has some harsh realities and should be a primary consideration when Canada examines the future of its economy and, particularly, its relationship with Japan. Resource businesses themselves obviously do not complain about continued Japanese interest in forest products, coal and other resources. For the country as a whole, however, continued dependence on resource exports, particularly when the long-term viability of resource supply in some sectors is in doubt, does not maximize Canadian jobs, increase diversification or improve national profitability.

Canada-Japan Trade in the Mid-1990s

The new trading conditions appear to have lasted only a decade. In 1994–95, the strength of the Japanese economy, working its way out of a prolonged slump, and the relative weakness of North American economies resulted in yet another currency crisis. The Japanese yen shot up in value, reaching postwar highs and adding further to the cost of Japan's export products; as of April 1995, $1 (Cdn.) could purchase only 60.53 yen, less than half the yen it could buy after the

Table 5
Balance of Trade, Canada's Trade with Japan
1980 – 1994
(in Cdn. $ millions)

Year	Surplus (+) or Deficit (-)
1980	1,560,674
1981	469,395
1982	1,041,592
1983	308,802
1984	-69,985
1985	-407,610
1986	-1,690,156
1987	-514,462
1988	-559,143
1989	-765,827
1990	-1,338,839
1991	-3,142,652
1992	-3,309,969
1993	-2,292,400
1994	-1,795,800

Source: *Canada-Japan Trade Council Newsletter* (March–April 1995).

revaluation of Japanese currency in 1985. The United States government escalated its attacks on the growing Japanese trade surplus with America, mostly in the politically symbolic automobile industry. Canada stood by, predictably silent in a conflict that promised to have significant effects on Canadian trade prospects. Japanese companies had attempted to counter American protectionist tendencies by moving a significant portion of their production to North America, thus offsetting the trade surplus figures, but this strategy was not enough. Through the spring of 1995, American officials demanded that Japan open its markets to automobiles made in the United States, and threatened full-scale trade retaliation if nothing was done.

Japan is facing yet another currency and trade crisis, sparked by its continuing success in the North American automobile market and by the strength of the yen relative to the American and Canadian dollars and other currencies. While some observers propose that this struggle will force Japan to make substantial economic changes, the lessons of the past suggest that these problems have long been anticipated by the Japanese, the demand to lower the trade surplus being far from new, and that greater Japanese attention to market opportunities in East Asia will offset part of the decline from the contretemps with the United States.

Volatility, therefore, characterizes the contemporary Japanese market, not least because of the increasing emphasis on producing for the nation's consumers. The rapid growth of East Asian economies has lessened the importance that Canada and other smaller trading partners play in the Japanese economic scheme of things, just as the development of additional supplies of resources reduces Canada's attractiveness as a place to invest and trade. Success in responding to Japan's changing needs will greatly influence Canada's success as a twenty-first century trading nation.

Without wishing to sound too cataclysmic, it may already be too late. While Canada has rested on the laurels of its postwar trading accomplishments, Japan has been seeking new markets in the industrialized and the developing world. East Asia—China, Vietnam, Indonesia, the Philippines, Hong Kong and Singapore—has the fastest-growing regional economy in the world. Japan has, for the past two decades, made significant efforts to expand its trading activity in this region, gaining a hammer-lock on the East Asian automotive and electronics industries and establishing a significant presence in most countries, with the exception of Korea, which has proven difficult to breach. Japanese automakers, both by trade and local manufacturing, control over 90 per cent of the market in Thailand, Indonesia and the Philippines, over 80 per cent of Hong Kong's trade and almost 70 per cent of Singapore's automobiles. In Malaysia, where Japanese auto-makers account for 48 per cent of all car sales, an almost equivalent percentage of vehicles are produced by Proton, a Malaysian company connected to the Mitsubishi Motor Corporation.

How important is Japan's shift in trading partners? Consider some very simple statistics: Less than a decade ago in 1986, 44 per cent of all Japanese exports came to North America, and 28 per cent went to Asia. By 1991, this trend had reversed: 30 per cent of all Japan's exports came to North America (to the tune of $107 billion), while 40 per cent went to Asia ($116 billion). While North Americans get riled about Japanese import restrictions on automobiles and rally the commercial troops for another round of self-destructive protectionism, Japan has been creating a new economic empire that focuses on the fastest-growing economies in the world, and it is gradually shedding its dependence on the once-glorious but stagnating North American trading zone. During the forty years after World War II, Japan desperately needed access to the North American markets and exploited them successfully. Canada and the United States remain important, but decisively less so—particularly Canada. North America will likely not receive the same level of attention that it did in the past.

Canadian Exports to Japan

Canada has not matched Japan's steadily increasing interest in the Asia Pacific region. In 1990, slightly more than 11 per cent of all Canadian exports went to this region; four years later, the total value of Canadian exports increased from $15.8 billion to $18.9 billion, but the region has actually declined in relative importance in terms of Canadian exports, to 8.8 per cent of the total. Imports from the Asia Pacific region have remained relatively stable, averaging between 13.8 per cent and 15.3 per cent of Canada's total. Canada now runs a sizeable and increasing trade deficit with the region, from $3.6 billion in 1990 to $9 billion ($1.8 billion of that accounted for by Japan) in 1994. With the solitary exception of Brunei (hardly a major international trading nation), Canada is currently running a trading deficit with all of its significant partners in the region.

Canada's performance as a trading nation improved dramatically from 1990 to 1994: exports rose from $141 billion in 1990 to $213 billion four years later, and imports increased from $136 billion to $202 billion. But the lion's share of the improvement has resulted from changes in Canada's relationship with the United States. While Japan has been busy cultivating new markets, Canada has been content to rework familiar soil. This strategy is risky, particularly given the changing dynamics of modern trade.

Japan is now Canada's second-largest trading partner and annually imports $8.5 billion worth of Canadian goods. Canadian exports to Japan continue to consist largely of resource products, although by 1991, sales of manufactured products exceeded 10 per cent of Japan's total imports from Canada. (See Tables 6 and 7.) Canada's

Table 6 Canadian Exports to Japan 1989 – 1994 (Cdn. $ millions, Customs Clearance Basis)	
Year	Total Value
1989	8,797,262
1990	8,186,387
1991	7,119,416
1992	7,452,222
1993	8,393,263
1994	5,113,807 (Jan. to July)
Source: Information provided by the Embassy of Japan in Canada (World Wide Web site).	

imports from Japan continue to grow at a more rapid rate than do exports to Japan. These imports still consist of high-cost manufactured goods, although, surprisingly, Canada also imports items such as fish and canned fruit.

An examination of several Canadian industry sectors and specific companies affords an opportunity to examine the evolving Canada-Japan trade relationship in greater detail. The variety of traders is substantial, from the unregulated pine mushroom business to the massive Quintette coal project, and indicates the range of Canadian trade relationships with Japan.

Forestry

Forestry is a key element in the resource economy of Western Canada, although the industry has recently faced disputes over clearcutting, general environmental issues and aboriginal land rights. Most large communities in British Columbia have one pulp and paper plant or sawmill (or both), northern Alberta has a vibrant industry, and thousands of residents in both provinces rely on forestry for employment. According to the Council of Forest Industries of British Columbia, Japan is that province's largest offshore export market, capturing 15.8 per cent of British Columbian lumber shipments in 1993, and it retains great growth potential (Table 8). Exports of forest

Table 7
Top Ten Canadian Exports to Japan
(Cdn. $ millions; Customs Clearance Basis)

Type of Goods	Amount
Lumber logs and plywood	2,216,000
Coal	1,205,000
Wood pulp	658,000
Fish and seafood	638,000
Canola	476,000
Copper	357,000
Chemicals	290,000
Wheat	287,000
Aluminum	272,000
Paper	267,000

Source: Information provided by the Embassy of Japan in Canada (World Wide Web site).

products to Japan from British Columbia in 1993 were valued at $2.6 billion, a sizeable portion of the province's total exports.

Individual companies have taken direct steps to respond to market opportunities in Japan. Several companies ensure that their lumber graders are trained for the Japanese market; thus, workers can grade the product in Canada before delivering it to Japanese markets. Mills that possess the Japanese certification stamp hope that this service will increase the marketability of their product to Japan.

Coal

Despite Canadian rhetoric about the importance of value-added industries, primary products remain the focus for much of Canada's trade with Japan. In the 1970s, representatives of Japanese steel mills were scouring the world, particularly Canada and Australia, in an effort to locate stable, long-term supplies of metallurgical coal (Tables 7 and 9). At the same time, the British Columbia government decided to pursue the rapid development of the vast metallurgical coal reserves in the northeastern part of the province. The juxtaposi-

Table 8
Dollar Value of British Columbia Forest
·Products Exports
1984 – 1993
(in Cdn. $ millions)

Year	Japan	Total
1984	906	6,025
1985	913	6,238
1986	1,126	6,961
1987	1,769	9,312
1988	1,912	9,838
1989	2,213	10,160
1990	1,790	9,272
1991	1,667	8,427
1992	2,038	9,524
1993	2,795	11,750

Source: Council of Forest Industries of British Columbia.

tion of these requirements and desires resulted in the development of the Northeast British Columbia Coal Project.

The Canadian government recognized that an assured long-term purchase commitment was necessary to make extraction of the coal reserves a viable option. For the Japanese steel mills an opportunity to enter into a long-term agreement and assure themselves of a guaranteed supply of coal was appealing. (Projections made in the early 1970s suggested that Japanese steel production could rise to 150 million tons per year by 1990, vastly exceeding the supply of raw materials then under contract to Japanese companies.)

The opportunity for a multiyear purchase agreement persuaded the federal and provincial governments to enter into a comprehensive development agreement with Quintette Coal Limited, the promoter of the Northeast Coal Project, to construct a $2.1-billion infrastructure system (of which over half the cost came directly from government coffers). Building the new company town of Tumbler Ridge

Table 9
Canadian Coal Sales to Japan
1992 – 1993
(million tonnes)

Year	Nova Scotia		Alberta		British Columbia		Canada	
	Total	Japan	Total	Japan	Total	Japan	Total	Japan
1992	2.1	0	8.7	6.0	17.4	9.7	28.2	15.7
1993	0.98	0	8.9	6.0	18.4	10.3	28.3	16.3

Source: Statistics Canada, *Coal Mines, 1993,* Catalogue 26-206.

cost $220 million. BC Rail built a 130-kilometre line from Anzac to Tumbler Ridge, spending more than $550 million in the process. (The opening up of two tunnels through the Rocky Mountains alone cost $156 million.) Canadian National Railway upgraded its facilities on the 960-kilometre line from Prince George to Prince Rupert, where the Ridley Island Seaport facility was built to load vessels destined for the docks of Japanese steel-makers. Including the cost of roads and boats, this new deep-water terminal cost $280 million.

The viability of the Quintette and Bullmoose mines (a smaller mining operation in the same area, operated and partially owned by Teck Corporation) depends on the fifteen-year supply contract and on continuing price stability for coal delivered under the contract. Unfortunately, by the time the mine opened, the price of coal had fallen. For the last ten years, Canadian producers and Japanese purchasers have been engaged in an ongoing debate over the appropriate price for the coal, a dispute that has called the mines' future into question. The saga is far from over, and hard feelings remain on both sides. To a number of Canadian observers, the coal procurement policies of the Japanese steel industry are somewhat manipulative. Critics argue that the Japanese steel industry deliberately encouraged excess capacity by offering long-term supply contracts at premium prices to many mines and then, after the market was flooded, attempting to renegotiate price and tonnage. The Japanese counter with the simple point that they had no idea that Japanese steel production would not reach the level anticipated in the 1970s and therefore would not require the coal initially anticipated or that world coal prices would decline markedly. However, as that is the case, they see no reason to pay prices dramatically higher than the world level. The Gregg River Mine is a $200-million, open-pit coal mine, located forty kilometres southwest of Hinton, Alberta. The mine, operated by Gregg River Resources, opened in April 1983 and produces 2.14 million tons of metallurgical coal annually for export to Japan. Coal production is dedicated to six Japanese steel mills under a fifteen-year coal-marketing agreement. Gregg River Resources, a subsidiary of Manalta Coal, operates the mine on behalf of an unincorporated joint venture between Gregg River Coal (which has 60 per cent ownership) and six Japanese steel companies and one Japanese trading company, each holding between 1.05 per cent and 13.98 per cent equity (to a total of 40 per cent).

Fish and Seafood

Canada has encountered reasonable success in its efforts to sell fish products to Japan. The Japanese market absorbs more than one-third of the world's total fish exports, making it the world's largest market for imported fish products. While about 65 per cent of Japan's demand for fish is met domestically, imports are steadily increasing in importance due to shrinking Japanese catches. In 1993, Japan imported 3.1 million tonnes of fish and fish products with a value of $14.7 billion (U.S.). Canada claims approximately 5 per cent of this market and ranks as the eighth-largest supplier of fish to Japan. As the value and volume of Japanese imports have grown, Canada has managed to keep pace, but has not increased its market share. A glance at British Columbia's north coast fishery reveals the importance of the Japanese market: Japan is either the primary or sole market for a substantial proportion of the fisheries in this area, including sockeye salmon (Japan accounts for 90 per cent of north coast sales), coho salmon (50 per cent), geoduck clams (100 per cent), sea cucumber (100 per cent), sea urchins (100 per cent), herring roe on kelp (100 per cent) and black cod (100 per cent). This degree of Japanese domination is not unique to northern British Columbia. In 1994, 95 per cent of Canada's sockeye exports went to Japan. The Japanese market continues to grow in importance with several of the key product lines, such as frozen coho and chinook salmon, and frozen and cured salmon roe, experiencing marked gains in 1994.

Aluminum

Canadian-based multinational corporations, such as Alcan Aluminium, have played a major role in the industrial and commercial development of the country, particularly after World War II, and, not surprisingly, led the country in developing and maintaining international business connections. Alcan's relationship with Japan began before World War I. The Japanese used aluminum as early as the 1890s for army mess kits, buckles and sabre clasps. However, with no bauxite and limited power resources, Japan did not begin aluminum smelting until the mid-1930s, when nationalist feelings prompted the government to subsidize the industry.

Until the 1930s, therefore, Japan relied entirely on imported aluminum, much of it from Canada. The second shipment from Alcan's smelter at Shawinigan, Quebec, went to Japan. This long-term relationship with Japan puts Alcan in a different category from virtually all other Canadian companies, whose business dealings are more recent. The longevity helps explain Alcan's willingness and ability to modify production to suit Japanese needs and the company's proactive role in facilitating connections with Japan (former Alcan president David Culver was the founding co-chair of the Canada-Japan Business Cooperation Council and current president Jacques Bougie is a director for the Asia Pacific Foundation and was a member of the Canadian panel that drafted the Canada-Japan 2000 report).

Alcan's current relationship with its Japanese customers is fostered and enhanced through its stakeholder interest in Nippon Keikenzoku K.K. (Nippon Light Metal or NLM). Alcan acquired a 50 per cent interest in this Japanese aluminum smelting company in 1952, and this relationship has allowed Alcan to maintain and improve its presence in Japan. (Japan established a number of large aluminum smelters which used oil-fired generators. The "oil shocks" of the 1970s drove the cost of running the smelters so high that Japan virtually gave up on aluminum smelting and turned the industry toward the manufacturing of aluminum products. Today, NLM operates the only aluminum smelting plant in Japan.) Alcan also has 49 per cent ownership of Toyo Aluminum, a Japanese producer of aluminum foil. Alcan Smelters and Chemicals is the largest employer in Kitimat, a community of approximately 11,000 people on the northwest coast of British Columbia. The Kitimat Works smelter opened in 1954 and started selling aluminum to the Japanese market in 1977. Currently, 58 per cent of the approximately 272,000 tons of metal produced annually at Kitimat Works is sold to Japan. In 1993, this proportion amounted to 167,400 tons of aluminum, sold at an average of $0.55 per pound, with a total value of $184.5 million (U.S.).

Pine Mushrooms

Japan has become well known in Canada for the quixotic culinary tastes of its population. Numerous foodstuffs of marginal significance in Canada, from whale meat and herring roe to geoducks (clams), have valuable markets in Japan. When Japanese companies have expressed interest in such products in Canada, Canadian entrepreneurs have been quick—too quick at times—to jump into the market. Pine mushrooms, to provide but one interesting example, fetch high prices in Japan where thin slices are used to flavor soups and other meals.

Pine mushrooms are harvested throughout British Columbia but most of the major harvesting areas are in the northern part of the province (near Terrace, the Nass valley, Bella Coola and Anahim Lake). Of these, the secluded forest groves of the Nass and Skeena valleys are recognized as superior pine mushroom harvesting areas. An estimated 5,000 to 10,000 pickers search the woods each year for the mushrooms. They earn an average of $44 a kilogram for top-grade pine mushrooms, although the price has soared as high as $986 a kilogram when crops in other countries, such as Korea, have dried up. Estimates of annual provincial production range from 50,000 to 500,000 kilograms per year, injecting an estimated $20 million annually into a handful of British Columbia communities.

Even though commercial pine mushroom harvesting has been carried out in British Columbia on a large scale for more than ten years, very little is actually known about the industry. No one paid much attention to the pine mushroom harvest until 1988. In that year, Japanese buyers pushed the price of mushrooms up to $100 per pound, sparking a "gold rush" fever in the Terrace-Hazelton region. Many local residents left well-paying jobs to cash in on the mushroom "bonanza," making thousands of tax-free dollars in the process. The harvest and sale of the business is completely unregulated and untaxed as pickers are paid under the table. In 1993, the provincial government appointed a task force to complete a review of the industry and make recommendations.

The provincial government's main goal is to ensure the long-term stability of the pine mushroom industry. Lack of regulation has meant violent encounters between rival pickers over the harvesting of territories (machine guns have been confiscated!), unsanitary conditions at giant picking camps, a deep concern that intense picking may be damaging the mushroom's ability to regenerate and the fear that logging is destroying mushroom patches. Ecologists believe that these mushrooms thrive because they grow among the trees. When forests are logged, the mushrooms disappear. So far, attempts to grow pine mushrooms outside their natural habitat have failed.

And so it goes through the Canadian resource economy. Japanese companies are attracted by the availability of abundant Canadian resources and resource products, from geoducks and coal to pine mushrooms and aluminum ingots. Canada has much to offer in this regard: political and economic stability, a highly skilled workforce, high-quality products, competitive prices and, because of these factors, long-term security of supply. These products carry an added benefit: they are "sourced" by Japanese traders anxious to ensure a steady flow of materials into the Japanese market and, compared to the highly competitive consumer trade, require relatively little product promotion.

Canadian companies attempting to break into the Japanese market face formidable barriers, not the least of which are culture and language. But having overcome those barriers, Canadian firms must make a sizeable, long-term commitment to Japan, for the doors (particularly for consumer goods) do not swing open easily and markets must be tended carefully. North American companies are not known for their forward-looking approach or their careful cultivation of potential customers; instead, a get-rich-quick mentality pervades the trading business, relying heavily on commercial gambles and expensive pop-culture advertising to develop market share.

Setting up shop in Japan is not easy, and there is certainly no guarantee of success. The country's myriad regulations and complex internal trading networks (involving warehouse operations and intermediaries) make market penetration difficult. Moreover, the costs of establishing a business in Japan are extremely high, especially in Canadian dollars. Robin Sears, a Canadian executive consultant specializing in Japan, recently forecast that it would cost $1 million (U.S.) for one year's operation of a small office with four or five employees, including one Japan-based North American, in Tokyo.

For Canadian firms, used to dealing with the familiar but volatile North American market, the unusual complexity and expense of doing business in Japan are formidable disincentives. With uncertain financial returns, cultural barriers and numerous linguistic and commercial challenges, it is of little surprise that Canadian business has tended to shy away from Japan. However, given the current and future importance of this market, Canada will continue to pay a high price for its comparative inability to break into Japanese trade.

Japanese Exports to Canada

Japan, in contrast, has experienced much less difficulty in finding a niche in the Canadian market. Because the Japanese place such an emphasis on the United States, Canada is relatively easy to understand (if only as a variation of America). Since World War II, Japanese business has been preoccupied with understanding and responding to the needs of the North American market place and has proven remarkably adept at penetrating this vast and wealthy economy. By working primarily through intermediary sales agents, including car dealerships and retail stores, Japanese manufacturers have been able to capture a significant portion of their target markets.

Canada imports a large volume of manufactured goods from Japan, having lost the trade surplus it maintained throughout most of its commercial history. (See Tables 3, 10 and 11.) The $10 billion worth of trade goods purchased from the Japanese represents a sizable portion of Canada's total imports. More important, Canada has come to rely heavily on Japan for manufactured and high-technology items. Long gone is the postwar tradition of purchasing huge quantities of cheap textiles and trinkets, with the label "made in Japan" being synonymous with second-rate production.

For the past twenty years, Japanese trade has been on the rise. Cars, car parts and trucks make up $4.1 billion of Japan's $10.7 billion in total trade. High-technology products, such as telecommunications equipment, computers and industrial machinery, make up the lion's share ($3.16 billion) of the remainder. "Made in Japan" now means high quality, cutting-edge technology, superb after-sales service and excellent value for money. The country and its trade goods have become synonymous with innovation, a vast jump from the postwar image of Japan as a nation of imitators and cut-rate producers.

The steady rise in the value of the yen has diminished the attractiveness of many Japanese trade goods, making it doubly fortunate

Table 10
Canadian Imports from Japan
1989 – 1994
($ millions; Balance of Payments Basis)

Year	Total Value
1989	9,563,089
1990	9,525,226
1991	10,262,068
1992	10,762,191
1993	10,689,823
1994	6,369,365 (Jan. to July)

Source: Embassy of Japan in Canada.

that the country's traders can rely on their reputation for high-quality production and highly desirable goods. Japan has responded by moving its manufacturing plants offshore, to low-wage countries in East Asia or to high-productivity producers such as Canada and the United States, where Japanese-owned companies can use domestic plants to skirt trade restrictions and preferences. When Canadians make a purchase from Toyota, the leading Japanese car manufacturer, that vehicle is more likely produced in Ontario, Kentucky or California than in Japan. A similar pattern has developed in computer and audiovisual manufacturing, with Japan now exporting its designs, manufacturing processes and marketing abilities, but relying on local producers and assemblers to put the final product together.

Over the past decade, Japan has undergone a fundamental commercial transition. Previously, the country produced for the Western, primarily North American, market, and refined and improved on products that had demonstrated a proven demand. More recently, Japanese manufacturers are targeting their wares at Japanese consumers, responding to their needs, tastes and expectations. When products prove successful in the Japanese market and when there appears to be an international demand, manufacturers trade them overseas. This strategy has resulted in a veritable explosion of consumer-driven innovation in Japan and has started a slow dissemina-

Table 11
Top Ten Canadian Imports from Japan
(Cdn. $ millions)

Type of Goods	Amount
Passenger Cars	2,264,000
Auto Parts	1,464,000
Telecommunications Equipment	1,227,000
Computers	1,192,000
General Machinery	1,010,000
Commercial Vehicles	339,000
Precision Instruments	280,000
Games and Toys	234,000
Transportation Equipment (excluding cars)	231,000
Televisions, Radios, Phonographs	216,000

Source: Embassy of Japan in Canada.

tion of products designed for, and tested in, the Japanese market. In the same way that the consumer revolution helped Westernize Japanese material culture earlier this century, there is the intriguing prospect that this Japanese-led revolution will slowly, and imperceptibly, "Japanize" Western societies.

Tourist Trade

Tourism, one of the world's fastest-growing economic sectors, has emerged as a central element in Canada-Japan commercial relations. The relationship is thus far massively one-sided, with only a handful of Canadians travelling to Japan and tens of thousands of Japanese tourists visiting Canada. The result has been a handsome trade surplus in Canada's favour that rests on Japan's fascination with Canada's wide open spaces and seemingly limitless frontier. Japanese travellers represented only 1.0 per cent of Canada's tourist trade in 1984 but grew to 2.7 per cent of all travellers in 1993. (The United States, in contrast, accounted for 87.1 per cent of visits in 1984 and

79.6 per cent in 1993.) Japanese travellers did, however, make up over 13 per cent of all non-American visitors in 1993.

The Japanese are not like others travellers, however. In 1993, 409,000 Japanese made trips to Canada, well over half (236,000) of whom came on vacation. They spread out fairly widely across the country, with British Columbia recording the largest number of visitors (227,000), followed by Ontario (149,000) and Alberta (122,000). Saskatchewan and Manitoba attracted fewer Japanese visitors (4,000 and 8,000, respectively), and the Atlantic provinces entertained around 11,000, many of them attracted to Prince Edward Island by the tales of *Anne of Green Gables*. (The total number of provincial visits exceeded the national total of 409,000 due to multiple stops by travellers.) Japanese visitors stayed, on average, seven days, the shortest stay of the non-American visitors. In comparison, European travellers remained in Canada for ten to thirteen days.

Japanese tourists are good for business. The Japanese spend more per trip ($1,103) than travellers from any other country, despite the relative shortness of their stays. European visitors spent, on average less than $1,000 per person during their (longer) trips to Canada. In fact, Japanese travellers spent an average of $156.60 per person per day, well in excess of the parsimonious Dutch ($54.10), British ($62.50) and Germans ($76.40). While the Japanese tend not to stay long in Canada, and typically stay within the confines of Japanese-run tour and hotel operations, they are big spenders.

Canadian travellers have been much less interested in Japan as a tourist destination, a tendency reinforced by the recent high value of the yen relative to the Canadian dollar. Conversion rates have knocked the bottom out of the affordable Japanese vacation: a small room in a modest Tokyo hotel can easily cost ¥15,000 ($245 at 1994 exchange rates), and even the price of a basic restaurant meal can be three to four times that of a comparable repast in Canada. While package tours reduce the overall cost considerably, Japanese travel is definitely not for the light of pocketbook. Canadians made a total of only 73,000 visits to Japan in 1993 (6,000 for a single night), which comprised only 1.4 per cent of Canadian travel abroad that year. Total Canadian spending reached $89.4 million.

The current imbalance in Canada-Japan tourist travel is likely to linger. Canadians remain strongly attracted to the United States and are particularly taken with winter retreats to Hawaii, Florida, the Caribbean and Mexico. They are not among the world's more adventurous travellers, a title that must go to the Germans, Australians and

New Zealanders, and thus have not been quick to respond to the enticements of the Orient. The Japanese, in contrast, are being encouraged by their government to take more leisure time and to increase their travel outside the country (partly to offset Japan's huge trade surplus). The Canadian wilderness and the Rocky Mountains hold considerable allure for Japanese travellers. An increasing number of Japanese companies have been investing in the hotel and travel sector in Canada, revealing once more the willingness of Japanese firms to see and seize opportunities. As has happened elsewhere, particularly in Hawaii and Australia, Japanese operators are moving to secure a large section of this lucrative business, controlling travel, hotel, retail and tours. The net result may well be a marked increase in Japanese tourist travel to Canada, but it is accompanied by increasing domination of that trade by Japanese-owned firms. It is becoming a familiar tale in Canada.

***

Canada's business future rests on the exploitation of international trading opportunities. While there have been success stories, the country's heavy reliance on trade in raw materials and partially processed resources should sound strong warnings to Canadians. Given the threat to Canada's resource stock, such as the debates over the harvesting of British Columbian forests and salmon stocks, the country should be worried about tying its economic future to the verities of the past. Corporate and regional successes in promoting Japanese trade notwithstanding, Canada has much work to do to hold its place, let alone expand its role, as a trading nation.

8

Canada-Japan Investment

Both Canada and Japan are significant players in the game of international investments. Canada has financed much of its decades-long flirtation with deficit financing by selling bonds and treasury bills outside the country (principally to the United States). Japan has purchased a substantial amount of foreign debt, using its massive stockpile of savings to become the world's greatest creditor nation. But international investments extend far beyond the now-extensive exchange of government and corporate paper. Canadian companies have invested billions of dollars in offshore corporations; many Canadian firms have large subsidiaries or branch-plant operations in other countries. Canadian mining companies have widely scattered investments, and capitalize on Canadian expertise to find lucrative properties throughout the world.

Japan has greatly expanded its international presence in recent years, using monies resulting from domestic prosperity and sky-high savings rates to fund corporate expansion that far exceeds the reach of its military during World War II. To avoid complex domestic trading regulations and protective tariffs, numerous Japanese firms have established subsidiaries around the world, opening manufacturing plants and expanding retail operations. Thus, Japanese automakers produce cars in Canada and the United States, and those vehicles circulate within North America under the trade liberalization of NAFTA. These companies have also set up plants in Britain, Europe and Southeast Asia, establishing an industrial presence in many countries.

The cross-border flow of money, in the form of direct investment, joint ventures, licensing agreements and less well-known portfolio investments (bonds, stocks and treasury bills) has been a key element in the globalization and liberalization of international trade. Borders have become remarkably porous as countries compete for investment capital and endeavour to attract new business. In the process, domestic economies have been transformed, with foreign-owned corporations emerging as major players. While economic nationalists bemoan the loss of control associated with large-scale foreign investment and high levels of foreign-held debt, others welcome foreign capital as an economic salvation.

Fewer than thirty years ago, Japan had a barely noticeable presence in the Canadian market place; now, the country plays a large role in several sectors and controls billions of dollars of Canadian stocks, bonds and investment properties. Canada has also been active in Japan, traditionally one of the world's toughest investment markets to crack, although not to the degree of Japan's involvement in Canada. Canadian firms have found a few good investments in Japan and solidified their hold on significant Japanese markets through direct investments. But the Japanese have shown themselves to be masters at this game: They have purchased or invested in crucial resource sectors, to ensure themselves of a steady supply of key Canadian materials. They have also built manufacturing plants to benefit from Canadian and American trade regulations, and discovered the value of capitalizing on Canadian labour, which is comparatively cheap, well trained and dependable, to overcome diseconomies created by Japan's soaring yen. In the process, the Japanese have emerged as primary players in the Canadian domestic economy, while limiting the role of Canadian (and other foreign) investors within Japan.

Japanese Direct Investment in Canada

The Japanese have traditionally invested in Canada to support their internal industrial requirements and to ensure a steady supply of key raw materials. Beginning early in the twentieth century but accelerating in the 1960s, Japanese companies invested in Canadian resources to guarantee their access to timber, minerals and food supplies. Forest products, copper and coal were the chief areas of investment, many of which came through joint ventures with Japanese trading companies (*sogo sosha*). In addition, Japanese companies often assumed minor equity positions in Canadian companies whose products they desired. Almost 50 per cent of the Japanese investment in Canadian resource development came in the form of loans, including corporate bonds and debentures. The amount of money involved was small, first because Japan was not particularly active in foreign investments before the 1960s and, second, because Canada was not yet deemed a prime investment market.

Table 12
Direct Foreign Investment in Canada
Selected Years, 1930 – 1990
(in Cdn. $ millions)

Year	Japanese Investment	Total Investment
1930	0	1,993
1940	0	2,064
1950	0	3,549
1960	0	11,230
1970	103	22,173
1980	605	51,240
1990	4,138	82,601

Source: Statistics Canada, Canada's International Investment Position: Historical Statistics, 1926–1992. Catalogue 67-202.

This initial "wave" of resource investment peaked in the early 1970s, when the Japanese shifted their emphasis to manufacturing. Their approach was very simple: they shipped components from Japan to be assembled in Canada, thus avoiding Canadian tariffs and other regulations. Japanese service companies, such as trading firms and banks, followed the investment dollars, setting up branches in Canada to support the export and import sectors. The level of Japanese investment exploded, from $605 million in 1980 to over $4.1 billion a decade later (see Table 12), largely in response to the trading opportunities with the United States created by NAFTA.

Through the 1980s, Japan's investment presence in Canada developed steadily. The country moved from being the eighth-largest foreign investor in Canada to being the third largest, behind the United States and the United Kingdom. From 1986, following the Plaza Accord, Japanese direct investment grew dramatically, although it paled in comparison to the massive American investments in the country ($5.8 billion compared to over $96 billion; see Table 13). Japanese investors began to abandon the traditional resource areas and move into a broader range of investments, including car

Table 13
Direct Investment in Canada by Japan and the United States
Selected Years, 1984 – 1994
(Cdn. $ millions)

Year	Total	Japan	United States
1984	85,964	2,074	64,762
1986	96,054	2,679	69,241
1988	114,480	3,582	76,345
1990	131,131	5,214	84,353
1992	138,492	5,802	89,013
1994	148,038	5,849	96,032

Source: Statistics Canada, *Canada's International Investment Position, 1994*, Catalogue 67-202.

assembly and auto parts manufacturing, the processing of wood fibre into newsprint, and such services as hotels, banking and construction. The patterns of Japanese investment changed in scale rather than in type, as Japanese branch plants in Canada went from producing primarily for the Canadian market to serving the much larger, richer North American market.

In the early 1980s, pulp and paper and mining were the primary recipients of Japanese investment capital. While investment in both areas declined after 1982, pulp and paper investment experienced a massive resurgence in 1987. (In fact, this sector accounted for 36 per cent of the increase in Japanese investment in manufacturing between 1987 and 1990.) After 1986, investment in the automotive, banking, and service sectors surged dramatically and, by 1990, these three sectors accounted for another 36 per cent of total Japanese investment in Canada. (See Table 15.)

While Japanese investments in Canada are significant to Canada, they represent only a fraction of Japan's total overseas investments. Table 14 indicates that Canada has received roughly $7.8 billion or 1.8 per cent of Japan's cumulative total overseas investment for the

Table 14
Japan's Foreign Direct Investment
Selected Countries, 1951 – 1993
(millions of dollars)

Country	1989	1991	1993	Cumulative 1951-1993
Australia	4,256	2,550	1,904	22,667
Brazil	349	171	419	7,614
Canada	1,362	797	562	7,769
China	438	579	1,691	6,163
Hong Kong	1,898	925	1,238	12,748
Indonesia	631	1,193	813	15,222
Netherlands	4,547	1,960	2,175	18,397
Singapore	1,902	613	644	8,481
United Kingdom	5,239	3,588	2,527	31,661
United States	32,540	18,026	14,725	177,098
Total	67,540	41,584	36,025	422,555

Source: *Canada-Japan Trade Council Newsletter* (September–October 1994).

fiscal years 1951 to 1993. In 1993, Canada was fourteenth on the list of Japanese foreign investment, receiving $562 million or 1.6 per cent of total Japanese investment. What is particularly striking is the amount of Japanese investment in other countries (see Table 14). Australia, with an economy smaller than Canada's, has received almost $23 billion or 5.4 per cent of the cumulative total and $1.9 billion or 5.3 per cent of total Japanese investment in 1993. A comparison between Canada and the United States is also instructive: in 1993, when Canada received $562 million or 1.6 per cent of total Japanese investment, the United States received $177 billion or 41.9 per cent. Therefore, Canada is receiving only 3.7 per cent of the North American total, which is greatly disproportionate for its share of the North American population. (This situation was not always the case. In the early 1980s, Japan's cumulative investment in Canada amounted to 9.7 per cent of the total invested in North America. By the end of the decade, however, this figure had dropped dramatically in relation to Japanese investment in the United States.)

Canadians point to the increasing level of Japanese investment as a sign of Canada's attractiveness; for example, Canadians applauded the recent announcement by Toyota of a major expansion of its Cambridge plant. However, the reality is very different. Japan has tied up important resource supplies (coal, forest products and minerals) through long-term contracts and loans, thus avoiding direct investment. More to the point, Japan has discovered that, save for a few key sectors such as the automobile trade, Canada's investment market is not particularly vibrant.

Accordingly, Japan has directed substantial portions of its investment capital to Southeast Asia, which houses the strongest growing economies in the world, and away from the more lethargic economic powers of North America. In 1989, Japan invested over $32 billion in the United States; four years later, that figure had fallen to less than $15 billion. Japanese investments in Canada fell from $1.4 billion in 1989 to $562 million in 1993. During this period, Japan substantially increased its investments in countries such as China and Indonesia.

The message for Canada is an important one: the second-largest economy in the world is losing interest in the Canadian market. Much of Japan's current interest, which is far from insignificant, rests on Canada's access to the United States, and not on the attractiveness of Canadian opportunities. Canada, however, appears to believe that continued Japanese investment is inevitable. If the patterns of the last half decade continue, however, Canada will find itself with limited access to the largest pool of investment capital in the world.

Canada may not be a particularly strong magnet for Japanese investment; however, it is important to consider those areas that have attracted interest. Japanese investment in Canada did not begin in earnest until the 1970s. Over the subsequent two decades, Japanese companies made sizeable investments in Canadian mines, oil and gas developments and pulp and paper. (See Table 15.) The Japanese also began to invest in the retail and manufacturing sectors, both of which expanded rapidly after the mid-1980s.

The pattern of Japanese investment changed dramatically after 1985. In the past decade, the Canadian government has reviewed 351

Table 15
Japanese Direct Investment by Industry in Canada
Selected Years, 1960 – 1990
(Cdn. $ millions)

Year	Manufacturing	Oil/Gas	Mining	Utilities	Retail	Finance	Other	Total
1961	1					1		2
1970	58	5	26		11	3		103
1980	159	49	68		257	27	45	605
1990	1,823	96	1	4	865	1,101	248	4,138

Source: Statistics Canada, *Canada's International Investment Position: Historical Statistics, 1926–1992*, Catalogue 67-202.

Japanese requests to invest under the Investment Canada Act. Cumulatively, these proposed investments called for $2 billion in new capacity and $5 billion in Japanese acquisitions of Canadian businesses. (Following a well-established trend in North America, the Japanese alloted more money to the acquisition of existing businesses than to the construction of new ones. The net benefit to the Canadian economy from these take-overs is debatable, although the infusion of additional capital and new commercial directions follow many such purchases.)

It would be wrong to leave the impression that the Japanese are backing out of commitments to Canada. Within those market niches that draw Japanese capital, the willingness to invest remains strong. The Japanese maintain major investments in companies such as the Alouette Aluminum smelter in Quebec and the 7-Eleven chain of convenience stores. Recently, a number of Japanese companies announced expansions of their operations in Ontario. Besides Toyota's planned expansion, the Japanese have announced additions to Honda's assembly plant in Alliston, Kao's computer diskette plant in Arnprior, a bearings plant in Mississauga and Omron's Oakville auto parts plant. Omron has also entered into partnership with Spectrum Signal Processing to make personal computer components. The news is not all positive, however. In 1994, Mitsubishi Electric Sales Canada Inc., Hitachi Canada Inc. and Sanyo Canada all announced

Table 16
Japanese Direct Investment by Industry in Canada
Selected Years, 1984 – 1994
(in Cdn. $ millions)

	1984	1986	1988	1990	1992	1994
Food, Beverages and Tobacco	9	9	15	38	24	25
Wood and Paper	73	93	788	1096	1187	856
Energy	709	715	251	-63	130	194
Chemicals and Textiles	15	1	7	220	240	226
Metallic Minerals& Metals	124	125	415	747	927	925
Machinery and Equipment	34	121	175	271	337	486
Transportation Equipment	348	768	815	757	898	955
Electrical	89	182	225	281	302	278
Construction	4	4		178	270	278
Transportation Services	5	5	16	50	16	50
Finance and Insurance	201	328	576	888	842	982
Consumer Goods and Services	372	197	100	368	285	286
Other	91	131	200	384	404	414
Total	2074	2679	3582	5214	5802	5849

Source: Statistics Canada, *Canada's International Investment Position, 1994*, Catalogue 67-202, Table 12.4.

the closing of television assembly plants in Canada and their transfer to larger facilities in the United States and Mexico.

Between 1985 and 1995, the range of Japanese investments in Canada broadened into new areas such as hotels and resorts, and existing commitments to the automobile industry deepened (see Table 16). Japanese investments in several key sectors, particularly pulp

Table 17
Japanese Corporations in the Top 500 in Canada in 1993

Rank	Name	Sales	Assets	No. of Employees	Percent Japanese Ownership
56	Mitsui Canada	$2.4b	$279m	125	100
60	Honda Canada	$2.2b	na	2,097	Honda 50
98	Toyota Canada	$1.4b	na	485	Toyota/Mitsui
104	Mitsubishi Cn	$1.3b	$176m	110	100
121	Marubeni Cn	$1.1b	$44m	81	100
133	Mazda Canada	$998m	$278m	220	Mazda 60
155	Nissan Canada	$854m	$501m	330	100
168	Nisho Iwai Cn	$780m	$30m	26	100
385	Crestbrook	$234m	$597m	1,150	Mitsui 27
411	Tomen Canada	$207m	$25m	na	100
433	Suzuki Canada	$190m	na	130	100
444	Yamaha Motor	$180m	$46m	180	100
488	Kamenatsu Cn	$144m	$19m	26	100
492	Sharp Elect	$142m	$84m	192	100

Source: Canadian Business 500, *Canadian Business*, June 1993.

and paper, reflected a continuation of the traditional pattern of ensuring control of essential resources. In other areas, such as finance, Japanese firms quickly established a significant presence, tied largely to their desire to service other Japanese companies in the Canadian market. By 1993, *Canadian Business'* Top 500 included fourteen Japanese-owned companies, dominated by the multifaceted Mitsui Canada operation and large-scale Honda and Toyota investments in the Canadian automobile sector (see Table 17).

Case Studies of Japanese Direct Investment in Canada

Investment statistics can be deceptive, suggesting a commonality of national purpose and control that may not actually exist. Capital follows opportunity (variously defined) and rarely operates under the tight strictures of national direction. Japan is something of an exception, given the close relationship between the government, the banks and the leading corporations. But even in Japan's case, investment statistics mask the fact that national investment portfolios represent the culmination of hundreds of separate corporate decisions. A brief analysis of Japanese investments in Canada by sector helps to illustrate this point.

Forestry, Pulp and Paper and Value-Added Products

The forest industry, though racked with controversy in recent years over logging practices, reforestation, and pollution levels in its mills, remains a vital economic sector in Canada. This area of Japanese investment, one of the most significant, also has one of the longest histories. Daishowa Paper Manufacturing Company, of Fuji City, is one of the world's top twenty pulp and paper producers in terms of sales and has been active in Canada for over twenty years. Daishowa was first attracted to Canada because it needed raw materials to supply its paper mills in Japan. (Today, 50 per cent of Daishowa's raw materials are supplied from abroad.)

Daishowa's involvement with Canada started with the purchase of wood chips, which were shipped to plants in Japan for processing. Then, in December 1969, the company set up a fifty-fifty joint venture with Weldwood of Canada, under the name of Cariboo Pulp & Paper Company, to build a bleached kraft pulp mill at Quesnel, British Columbia. In 1981, Daishowa and Vancouver-based West Fraser Mills established the Quesnel River Pulp Company, a fifty-fifty joint venture producing thermomechanical pulp for Daishowa's newsprint machines.

Japanese companies also have a commanding interest in Crestbrook Forest Industries, which operates three sawmills and a softwood pulp mill in southeastern British Columbia and has a 40 per cent interest in the Alberta-Pacific joint venture in northern Alberta (discussed below). This large company, with over 1,100 employees, is owned by the Honshu Paper Company (26.7 per cent), Mitsubishi Corporation (26.7 per cent) and the Ontario Municipal Employees Retirement Board (17.3 per cent). The company's sawmills at Canal Flats, Elko and Cranbrook produce lumber and value-added products for the Canadian and American markets. The pulp mill at Skookumchuck produces softwood kraft pulp for use in the production of fine writing paper. All pulp is purchased by Honshu Paper and Mitsubishi for resale.

Japanese companies remain strongly interested in Canadian forest products. The recent establishment of two pulp mills in northern Alberta, by Japanese multinationals eager to secure long-term supplies of high-quality fibre, created tremendous local controversies and resulted in a substantial reorientation of the region's economy. In 1988, Daishowa finalized an agreement allowing it to construct a $580-million bleached kraft pulp mill with a daily capacity of 1,200 tons near the town of Peace River. The Japanese company signed a renewable twenty-year forestry management agreement to harvest an area of more than 24,000 square kilometres. The provincial government also agreed to spend $65 million on infrastructure costs (road and rail access), including a portion of the expenses incurred in building a new bridge to be used solely by the mill. The mill opened in September 1990.

Alberta-Pacific (a joint venture of three primarily Japanese-owned entities, with Mitsubishi Corporation being the dominant interest) concluded an agreement with the Alberta government in August 1991 to construct a $1.3-billion bleached kraft pulp mill. The mill was designed to produce 1,500 tons of pulp per day and was built between Athabasca and Lac La Biche. The Japanese joint ventures, under a renewable twenty-year agreement, obtained the management rights for establishing, growing and harvesting deciduous and coniferous trees in a 61,000-square-kilometre area of northeast Alberta. In addition, the Alberta government, while not taking an equity position in the project, agreed to invest $275 million in subordinated debentures in the three companies. The government also invested about $50 million in roads, rail lines and other infrastructure. (The Alberta government invested this money despite clear evidence that inducements were not necessary; the Japanese simply wanted access to the timber.) In total, the land to which these Japanese multinationals have management rights amounts to approximately 8 per cent of the province of Alberta.

Japanese investments in forest products have expanded beyond traditional sectors such as lumber, wood chips and pulp and paper. The Canadian Chopstick Manufacturing Company established what it calls "the largest chopstick plant in the world" in Fort Nelson, a community of about 5,000 people in the northeastern corner of British Columbia. The company is registered in Canada and is owned by

Mitsubishi Canada (45 per cent) and Chugoku Pearl and Company (55 per cent), a Japanese manufacturer of plastic fast-food containers. In May 1989, Canadian Chopstick received $1.1 million in repayable loans from each of the federal and provincial governments to help with construction and equipment costs. The company hired about 210 people from the Fort Nelson area to staff the $15-million project and, in April 1990, began producing semifinished chopsticks to sell overseas, primarily to Japan. The company now produces 9 million pairs of chopsticks daily, is one of the biggest employers in Fort Nelson and pumps about $5 million annually into the town's economy. Loggers and truckers now work year-round, supplying wood to the plant.

Other value-added forestry companies have appeared in recent years. Mitsui Homes, the largest Japanese builder of prefabricated and two-by-four homes, has long maintained strong trading connections with various British Columbia lumber companies. In 1993, Mitsui Homes departed from the long tradition of exporting Canadian raw materials for processing in Japan by establishing a manufacturing plant in Langley, British Columbia, which produces prefabricated homes that are shipped to Japan for assembly. Mitsui Homes was, interestingly, attracted by the comparatively low cost of the highly trained Canadian workforce; low labour expenses enabled the company to reduce production costs.

Automobiles and Auto Parts Manufacturing

In the public eye, no economic sector is more strongly associated with the Japanese than automobile manufacturing. For those who remember the first Datsun (Nissan) vehicles and pint-size Honda Civics and who wondered if anyone would buy them, this development is particularly ironic. Over the past two decades, Japanese automobile manufacturers have set the industry standard, particularly for innovative designs, good quality and high levels of service. The signing of NAFTA, combined with the earlier Autopact (Canada–United States Automotive Products Agreement), ensure Canadian producers preferential access to American markets. It is this opportunity and the increasing protectionist pressures in North America, much more than the intrinsic attractiveness of investing in Canada, that have lured the Japanese automakers.

There are three Japanese-owned auto production plants in Canada: Honda Canada, Toyota Motor Manufacturing Canada and CAMI Automotive (a Suzuki–GM Canada joint venture). All three are lo-

Table 18
Japanese Automotive Parts-Related Investment and Joint Ventures in Canada

Auto Parts Manufacturers

Company	Number of Employees	Year	Location	Product Line
ABC Nishikawa (J)	150	1989	Ont.	Instrument panels
Atoma International (J)	2,500	1989	Ont.	Parts,electrical components
Bellemar Parts (J)	76	1988	Ont.	Seat assemblies
Bridgestone (D)	2,150	1990	Ont.	Tires
Can. Auto Parts (D)	155	1984	B.C.	Aluminum wheels
DDM Plastics (J)	750	1989	Ont.	Panels, dashboards
F&P Mtg. (J)	380	1987	Ont.	Support beams, suspension parts
General Seating (J)	289	1989	Ont.	Seating
Lear Seating (L)	1,663	1984	Ont.	Seat frames
MSB Plastics (D)	120	1989	Ont.	Mould components
Nichrin (D)	212	1987	Ont.	Hosing, binding
NTN Bearing Mtg. (D)	110	1973	Ont.	Bearings
Omron Dualtech Auto Electronics (D)	150	1984	Ont.	Auto relays
Progressive Moulded Products Ltd. (L)	210	1984	Ont.	Cooling fans
Quality Safety (J)	669	1987	Ont.	Seat belts
Rockwell International Suspension Systems (J)	230	1986	Ont.	Suspension systems
Vuteq Canada Corp.(D)	160	1989	Ont.	Window shields
Waterville T.G. (J)	1,340	1986	Que.	Weather strips
Woodbridge Inoac (J)	120	1986	Ont.	Seat forms, panels
Yachiyo of Ontario (D)	90	1990	Ont.	Stamping,welding, painting, assembly

(continued)

Table 18 continued Materials and Machine Tools				
Company	Number of Employees	Year	Location	Product Line
Aclo Compounders (J)	65	1986	Ont.	Thermoplastic
Amada Promecam (D)	15	1987	Ont.	Metal fabricating
Canada Mold Tech. (J)	47	1989	Ont.	Dies
DNN Galvanizing (J)	102	1993	Ont.	Galvanized steel
Sanyo Machine Works (D)	45	1982	Ont.	Auto assembly line equipment
Tsubaki of Canada (D)	76	1971	Ont.	Assembly equipment chassis,sprockets
Z-Line (Stelco) (J)	55	1990	Ont.	Coated steel
J=Joint Venture; L=Licence Agreement; D=Direct Investment (wholly-owned)				

Source: Pacific Automotive Co-operation Inc. (PAC), Tenth Anniversary Report: 1984–1994, in JAMA Canada Annual Report, 1994.

cated in southern Ontario, in Alliston, Cambridge and Ingersoll, respectively. Honda's plant started operations in November 1986, followed by Toyota two years later and the Suzuki–GM Canada joint venture in 1989. These three plants produced 343,000 units in 1993, about 15.3 per cent of total Canadian motor vehicle production. Over 85 per cent of all vehicles produced at these plants are destined for export, mainly to the United States.

The Honda, Toyota, and CAMI plants represent a combined investment of $1.4 billion, and employ 5,050 people at full production. These numbers promise to grow. In November 1994, Toyota announced a $600-million expansion at its Cambridge plant. The new facility will produce 120,000 additional Corolla sedans per year, bringing total plant production to 200,000 cars annually. Toyota's workforce is expected to grow from 1,000 to approximately 2,200 employees. Honda also has plans to increase its plant's capacity from 101,000 vehicles to 120,000 vehicles, with the production of a new Acura passenger car for the Canadian market. These additions mean that, by 1997, total Japanese auto investment will have reached $2 billion and will employ over 6,200 people.

Supporting these three manufacturing plants are over twenty machine tool operations and manufacturers of auto parts and related materials in Canada (see Table 18). Pacific Automotive Cooperation was formed in 1984 to facilitate further Japanese investment in this sector, particularly by supporting joint ventures between Canadian and Japanese firms.

Major Hotel and Resort Property Purchases

Japanese companies have been quick to capitalize on growing Japanese fascination with Canadian tourist attractions (particularly in British Columbia and Alberta). In the 1980s, Japanese tourism to Canada increased dramatically, followed closely by a surge in Japanese property investment. In British Columbia, Japanese companies own a number of hotels in Vancouver, the Coast Hotel chain, five of the twenty-six hotels at Whistler Mountain, and a number of other properties in resort locations (see Table 19). They also own major hotels in Banff, Alberta, and in Niagara Falls, Ontario, and the Sheraton Hotel in Hamilton, Ontario. (While the Japanese have invested in hotels, resorts and a few condominium developments, they have not purchased many offices, shopping centres or family homes, in sharp contrast to the high-profile pattern of Hong Kong investments in the Vancouver region. Sun Enterprises of Tokyo's purchase of the Hong Kong Bank of Canada building in Vancouver for $130 million in 1989 is one exception to this pattern.)

The Japanese Banking and Securities Sectors in Canada

For many years, Canadian finance was largely closed and tightly regulated. Foreign banks operated under severe constraints, and most avoided major activities in the country. Changes to the Canadian Bank Act in 1981 substantially deregulated the industry and drew numerous foreign banks into Canada. Twelve Japanese banks had established representative offices in Canada before 1981; between 1982 and 1987, eleven of these established full-fledged subsidiary operations. The Japanese banks focused almost entirely on wholesale commercial banking for larger Canadian companies and for Japanese

Table 19
Major Canadian Hotel and Resort Properties
Purchased by Japanese Investors
1986–1990

Year	Japanese Investor	Hotel/Resort Name	Location
1986	Tokyu	Pan Pacific	Vancouver
1987	Itoman	Harrison Hot Springs	Harrison
1988	Aoki	Westin Hotel	Vancouver
1988	Listel	International Lodge	Whistler
1988	IPEC\ICEC	Nancy Green Lodge	Whistler
1988	IPEC	Harbour Towers Hotel	Victoria
1988	Mutsumi	Whistler Fairways Hotel	Whistler
1988	Okabe	Coast Hotel/Motel chain	Vancouver
1988	Okabe	Ramada Renaissance Hotel	Vancouver
1989	Palios	O'Douls Hotel	Vancouver
1989	Chotokan	Radium Hot Springs Resort	Radium
1989	Yamanouchi	Chateau Whistler (80%)	Whistler
1989	Pharmaceutical Crossroads	Royal Oak Inn	Victoria
1990	Enterprises Libest	Westbrook Whistler	Whistler
	Seibu	Toronto Prince Hotel	Toronto
	Okabe	Coast Bastion Inn	Nanaimo
	Sumitomo Trust Affiliate	Rimrock Resort Hotel	Banff

corporations in Canada. According to David Edginton, a Canadian geographer specializing in the study of Japanese business activity, as of 1986, Canadian subsidiaries of Japanese banks handled close to

90 per cent of Japanese financial business in Canada. The Japanese pattern of keeping within the group now extended to the raising of capital for investments in Canada.

Canada continued to deregulate its tightly bound financial sector. Significant changes in the Ontario Stock Exchange Law in 1987 resulted in several Japanese securities firms (Nomura, Nikko, Daiwa, Yamaichi and Sanyo) establishing offices in Canada. These firms played several specific roles: helping Canadian companies and governments gain access to the vast Japanese capital pool, marketing Canadian bonds to major Japanese investors (including insurance companies and pension fund managers) and selling Japanese securities to Canadian interests, particularly the large pool investors (pension and trust funds).

Canadian Investment in Japan

Canadians have enthusiastically welcomed recent Japanese investment and come to rely on a continued infusion of foreign capital to buttress the nation's resource and manufacturing base. Canadian businesses, however, have become more reluctant to invest in Japan, due to the more restricted nature of its economy and Canada's inability to break through the cultural, linguistic and commercial barriers. While Japanese investment in Canada in 1990 amounted to $4.6 billion (U.S.), Canadian investment in Japan in 1989 totalled a mere $393 million, a tiny portion of the almost $8 billion that Canadians invested overseas that year. Canadians invested over $5 billion (U.S.) in the United States in 1990, accounting for two-thirds of Canada's total overseas investment. Examination of Canada's entire overseas portfolio reveals cautious investment strategies with an emphasis on English-speaking countries. In 1989, Australia, a minor economic power compared to Japan, attracted $2.1 billion in Canadian investment; Singapore, an Asian but English-speaking country with strong British/Commonwealth connections, secured $1.3 billion in Canadian investment.

Canadians are not alone in avoiding direct investment in Japan, nor is their limited investment necessarily due to a reluctance to invest. For years, MITI and the Japanese ministry of finance have worked hard to restrict foreign investment, fearing difficulty for the government in monitoring foreign companies and wishing to avoid the possibility of corporate profits being invested outside Japan.

In 1994, Japan attracted only $3.1 billion (U.S.) in overseas investment, of which the United States accounted for 30 per cent. On

Table 20
Foreign Direct Investment in Japan
(millions of U.S. dollars)

Fiscal Year	Number of Cases	Amount (U.S. $)
1951–1980	8,826	2,979
1982	1,052	749
1984	3,685	493
1986	3,079	940
1988	4,268	3,243
1990	5,939	2,278
1991	4,212	4,339
1992	1,271	4,084
1993	1,072	3,078

Source: *Canada-Japan Trade Council Newsletter* (July–August 1992) and *FIND Annual Report, 1994.*

a worldwide basis, Japan accounted for a minuscule 0.7 per cent of total foreign direct investment; the United States on its own attracted 22 per cent and the European Union, 38 per cent. Canada ranked fifth among countries investing in Japan, with a 4.9 per cent share. The small amount of direct foreign investment is somewhat surprising, given Japan's status as a major international player. (See Tables 20 and 21.) However, the logistics of the Japanese market—soaring real estate costs, difficulty recruiting qualified personnel, language and cultural barriers and limited international knowledge of the intricacies of Japanese business—help explain this discrepancy.

The value of Canadian investment in Japan is deceptively impressive. While a few Canadian firms have made substantial investments in Japan, a sizeable portion of this funding actually represents the repositioning of investments among subsidiaries. In 1991, for example, Canadian direct investment in Japan soared by $764 million (U.S.), representing 17.6 per cent of all foreign direct investment in the country that year. However, this increase was tied to the reallocation of capital accounts between companies and their subsidiaries.

Table 21
Canadian Direct Investment in Japan
Selected Years, 1920 – 1990
(In Cdn. $ millions)

Year	Investment in Japan	Total Direct Investment
1920	1	212
1930	1	443
1940	1	681
1950	–	990
1960	15	2,468
1970	48	6,188
1980	109	26,967
1990	770	87,886

Source: Statistics Canada, *Canada's International Investment Position: Historical Statistics, 1926–1992.* Catalogue 67-202.

The actual level of Canadian-controlled direct investment in Japan was considerably smaller.

In any event, some companies have taken the investment plunge into the complex and difficult Japanese market. Many are in the resource sector, building on long associations with Japanese partners. Among these active companies are Alcan Aluminium, Falconbridge, Inco and MacMillan Bloedel. Canada Packers, with heavy involvement in meat sales, has established offices in Japan, along with Canadian Airlines International and Moore Business Forms. Several high-technology firms, including Northern Telecom, Newbridge Systems and Cognos, have also recently set up operations in the country.

While direct investment in Japan remains relatively small, Canadian capital has been at least as active, and probably more so, on an international scale than Canadian trade. Canada had, after all, $125 billion in foreign investments in 1994, although a large proportion was in the United States. Canada has been a stable and active player in the world's capital markets, aided by the size and competence of

Table 22
Canadian Direct Investment in Japan and the United States
Selected Years, 1984 – 1994
(in Cdn. $ millions)

Year	Japan	United States	Total
1984	312	34,700	50,092
1986	461	42,027	61,497
1988	482	48,809	76,169
1990	919	55,475	91,462
1992	2,632	61,806	107,240
1994	3,030	67,739	125,247

Source: Statistics Canada, Canada's International Investment Position, 1994 Catalogue 67-202.

its main financial institutions, and has gradually established a global presence. As suggested earlier, however, this presence tends to be strongest in English-speaking countries and appears to be systematically deterred by the barriers of language and culture. With this trend, Canadian financial markets are simply replicating a pattern that runs through the nation's business affairs.

***

Canadian nationalists have, since the 1960s, decried the level of foreign ownership of Canadian resources and, therefore, foreign domination of the Canadian economy. Most of the anger and concern focuses on the United States, and rightly so, for American control of the Canadian economy is indeed extensive. While Japan's role has increased in importance in recent years, it pales in comparison to that of the United States.

Within the baffling array of investment figures and statistical trends, several vital elements stand out. Canadian companies have made only minor inroads into the Japanese economy, following an international tendency to shy away from the complex Japanese investment market. In terms of Japanese investment, Canada is a fiscally dependent country, perhaps to a dangerous extent. In addition, the Japanese have bought into several key resource sectors, ensuring themselves of a long-term supply of inexpensive Canadian raw materials and limiting the potential value-added benefits that might accrue to Canada (if it ever took concerted action on this front). Japan currently has a high-profile presence in Canada, in the form of several major factories, resort hotels and controversial forestry projects.

In the midst of this expanded investment picture rests a serious and looming problem: either Japan is losing interest in Canada, or Canada's attractiveness is fading (in all but a few key sectors, such as automobile manufacturing). Millions of dollars of investment capital that previously made its way to North America will now solidify economic connections between Japan and Southeast Asia, a development which portends future difficulties for both Canada and the United States. Japan has chosen to turn its attention to the rapidly growing economies of Asia and away from the turgid, slow-moving North American scene; Canada has not yet fully recognized the fundamental importance of this choice.

How important is this transition? It is almost impossible to estimate the cost of opportunities lost, for it is difficult to predict what would have happened had Japan retained its strong interest in Canadian investments. The current situation is hardly of crisis proportions, because Japanese capital continues to flow into established sectors. Hence, the real cost is probably symbolic: one of the world's great economic powers appears to have decided that Canada will not be one of the focal economic players of the twenty-first century. Because Canada is still rich, in terms of resources and labour, and because Canadian producers have excellent access to the American market, investment will continue to flow into Canadian companies. But the search for commercial innovation, productivity gains, expanding markets and profit has led the Japanese from Vancouver, Toronto and Ottawa, to Singapore, Taiwan, China and Indonesia.

The pattern of Japanese investment may well be the canary in the cage for the Canadian economy, an early warning sign that all is not well. In fact, alarm bells should be ringing throughout government and business circles, in response to indications that Canada's prosperity rests on shaky ground. While Canada has clearly opted for closer commercial and economic ties with the United States, the benefits of which remain hotly debated across the country, observers would profit from an examination of developments with the country's second most important economic partner. If investment is an economic surrogate for intimacy, then the Canada-Japan love affair appears to be cooling down. And if, as many economic observers are forecasting, Japan and the Far East hold the key to economic growth in the next century, the deterioration of this commercial relationship (in spite of strengthening diplomatic and cultural ties) holds worrisome implications for Canada.

9

The Future of the Canada-Japan Business Relationship

Canada has become a trade-dependent economy without a deep-seated trading culture. We have developed a nation of managers rather than entrepreneurs. Our socio-cultural values emphasize risk-evasion rather than risk-taking. Our conservative ethos makes us resistant to rapid adjustment and revolutionary changes. We see problems rather than opportunities. These values may have served us well during a period of stability, but they are ill-suited to a period of accelerating and pervasive change.

—Michael Hart,
*What's Next: Canada, the Global Economy
and the New Trade Policy*

In the rapidly changing world of international business and trade, it is extremely difficult to predict trends and trading patterns. The nature of the relationship between Canada and Japan is particularly hard to forecast. Trade between the two countries continues to grow, although generally within established patterns, even though Japan's approach to international business has changed dramatically. And both Canada and Japan are experiencing profound internal transformations, from Canada's new-found fiscal conservatism and continued struggles with Quebec separatism to Japan's political corruption scandals and recent crises in major financial institutions.

One element of vital importance remains: Canada-Japan trade is far more crucial to Canada than to Japan. Therefore, it is in Canada's interest to maintain, expand and strengthen ties with its second-largest trading partner. There is limited evidence to date that Canada has succeeded in doing so, and even less of an indication that the country has the political, commercial and financial will to develop a consistent national approach to its trade relationship with Japan. Canada must determine the degree of commitment it wishes to make to the Japanese market and then evaluate the effect of Japan's transformations on Canadian business; finally, Canada must take the dramatic, long-term steps necessary to capitalize on opportunities in Japan. Canada can, of course, choose not to make these changes in its approach, but this position would exact a considerable national price.

The Importance of Japan as a Trading Partner

As a first order of business, Canada must decide how important it believes Japan will be as a trading partner. The recent Japanese recession has convinced many Canadians, including the prime minister, it seems, that their country's future is best tied to China—the sleeping economic giant of the Orient. Over the past year, the changing value of the yen, the consequent increase in the cost of Japanese exports and competition from other countries have signalled to many observers that Japan's sprint to the front of the economic pack is doomed to come up short. Crises in several key financial institutions and a spate of bad economic news reinforce this image. This argument holds allure for most Western observers who do not wish to believe that Japan can create another economic miracle and who maintain that the American-driven order is inherently superior. Certainly for Canadians, Japan's current difficulties provide justification for those who believe that Canada should not make the concerted effort and the commitments necessary to flourish in the Japanese market.

But many others believe that Japan's ascendancy is far from over and argue that the country's remarkable economic surge will continue into the twenty-first century. *The Japan That Can Say No*, an economic and political polemic by Shintaro Ishihara, touched nerves in North America. Ishihara, a Japanese parliamentarian, insists that racism is at the root of America's inability to learn from Japan's success, that growing Japanese self-confidence will fuel global expansion, and that Japan will soon surpass the United States to become the world's largest economy. The latter view is also presented in a recent best seller, *Blindside: Why Japan is Still on Track to Overtake the U.S. by the Year 2000*, by long-time Asia watcher Eamonn Fingleton. The author argues that Western observers consistently misrepresent Japan's success, underestimating the scale of economic growth and misreading the source of the country's sustained expansion. He asserts that "by pumping its huge savings single-mindedly into a narrow range of high-growth monopolistic industries, Japan's economic leaders can realistically aim to control the world's economic future" (p. 34). The country has ruthlessly cut back on unprofitable businesses, with the important cultural exception of agriculture, and targeted resources on more dynamic sectors. Fingleton concludes that the Japanese economy will continue to grow, baffling observers who forecast a serious recession, and will indeed overtake the American economy.

(The difference between the Japanese and Canadian approaches hardly needs to be pointed out. Canada has historically propped up inefficient industries for political reasons, poured millions of dollars into ill-advised development projects, lauded the importance of small business as the "engine" of economic growth and tolerated intense business competition, including that between provinces. The federal government's record of shaping economic development is very poor—witness the massive amounts of money dispatched to the Maritimes in a largely unsuccessful attempt to create a solid economic base—and reveals none of the control and prescience of the Japanese system.)

Close followers of the Japanese economy caution that previous forecasts of Japan's imminent collapse have been grossly inaccurate. They point out Japan's proven ability to adapt and respond quickly to changing circumstances—a characteristic not shared by Canada. Kenneth Courtis, a strategist and senior economist for the Deutsche Bank Group in Asia, believes that Japan will emerge stronger from the current economic slowdown and continue to outperform the West into the next century. He argues that the recession of the early 1990s was policy-induced and that Japan has learned to do more with less. This rationalization, he feels, will make Japan even more competitive in the future. These changes foreshadow significant opportunities and challenges for Canadian business. One fundamental transition was the shift from product innovation directed at North American consumers to product innovation aimed at Japanese consumers.

Japan's Innovation-Based Economy

Japanese-centred commercial innovations are transforming the tastes and habits of Japanese consumers and presenting both a radically different market for importers and new opportunities for exporters seeking a niche in North America. A number of interesting products are doing well in Japan but have not yet been exported to other countries. Items such as the head-cooling pillow for hot summer nights, *zabu zabu* balls (added to the washing machine to facilitate cleaning), refrigerators with five or six compartments, each with a different cooling system for a different kind of food, and a machine to discourage obscene phone calls (push a button and a threatening male voice yells out or a 100 decibel blast shrieks into the caller's ear) show considerable consumer potential for other markets.

Other larger and more commercial products include temporary sidewalks (standard modular concrete curb pieces which are inexpensive and easy to install and therefore useful during road construction projects), a car wash that takes up only 360 square feet, automated downtown parking towers (a Ferris-wheel-style elevator rotates cars and empty spaces up and down the parking tower) and capsule office buildings and hotels (with individual working or sleeping compartments).

Unique food and restaurant ideas are also commonplace in Japan. Consumers can buy apples inscribed with personal messages that have been grown into the fruit, ice cream with flavours such as sweet potato, blue cheese, basil leaf and oolong tea, spaghetti sandwiches, hot cocoa with chili sauce, pizza with corn and tabasco sauce and curry donuts. Theme restaurants (with multicourse meals, all including one ingredient, such as garlic), bars where you pay for the time spent, not the alcohol consumed, restaurants where noodles float down a chute in front of customers who grab them with their chopsticks and cook-it-yourself restaurants are a few examples of unique Japanese establishments.

Vending machines dot nearly every street corner in the country and supply almost any product imaginable. Most vending machines sell candy, pop, beer, whisky and hot and iced coffee and tea in cans, but machines also sell pantihose, rice, magazines, videos, milk, condoms, french fries, magnifying glasses, shaving cream, horoscopes and even frozen vacuum packages of beef.

There is little evidence that Canadian business is looking seriously at the wave of product innovation currently underway in Japan. So accustomed are North Americans to seeing Japan as the source of high-quality manufactured products such as cars, audio equipment and computers, that they have made comparatively little effort o identify other Japanese products for potential importation. Japan has an unparalleled ability to satisfy niche markets and a strong service orientation. Canadian business could benefit from learning about the

Japanese experience, being in touch with the fast-moving innovations in consumer products, and developing a trading relationship designed to bring Japanese products to North America.

Japan and the North American Free Trade Agreement

One of Canada's greatest wild cards, particularly when considering Japanese direct investment, is NAFTA. B. Anne Craib, government relations analyst with the Japanese Economic Institute in Washington D.C., observed, "Now that the agreement is actually in effect, one question that is little analyzed in the United States but of interest in Japan, as well as Canada, is whether NAFTA ultimately will create incentives for Japanese businesses to operate in Canada, or whether other factors will intervene to limit their Canadian benefits in NAFTA markets for some time" (Canada-Japan Trade Council *Newsletter*, 1995). Canadians hope that because of the Canada–United States Free Trade Agreement and NAFTA, Japanese firms will invest in Canada as a means of serving the North American market. Japanese investment will be drawn to Canada's access to the American market, the social welfare net (now under attack but an effective means of spreading the cost of supporting workers from the company to society at large) and lower input costs (particularly regarding land and energy). Canada's attractiveness could be particularly enhanced if American concern about foreign, and specifically Japanese, ownership of primary industries or properties leads the United States to make foreign investing awkward or difficult. Japanese firms that invest in both Canada and the United States are spreading the risk; they can thus operate in separate political and legal jurisdictions, both with access to the continent's vital markets.

The generally favourable impression received by the Morohashi Investment Mission, which visited Canada in October–November 1989, is another encouraging sign. The mission's report allayed some of the Japanese business community's concerns over the Canada–United States Free Trade Agreement. (Some feared that the agreement would result in the creation of "Fortress North America" and that it would be used against Japanese business). The mission also noted that while "an increasing rejection of Japanese investment had been observed in the United States, Canada still welcomed direct investment from Japan." Canada also has a favourable image in Japan. The Japanese generally perceive the country to be safer and more welcoming than the United States. Canada is not tainted with the stereotype of violence and racism attributed to the United States.

Those Canadians who are less optimistic about the free trade agreements fear a dramatic decrease in Japanese investment in Canada. They argue that Japanese companies will choose to build plants in the United States where costs are lower and the market is larger, and the issue of trade imbalance is more politically charged. In addition, Japanese firms are nervous that their Canadian subsidiaries could be denied access to the American market because of protectionism. This nervousness follows an incident in 1992 involving Honda. United States Customs ruled that 100,000 of Honda's Canadian-produced Civics did not meet the content regulations spelled out in existing trade agreements. Although United States Customs did not succeed in collecting back taxes as it wished, the episode damaged Canada's reputation for providing a safe environment for foreign investment.

Canada's Competitors

On a broader level, Canadians are discovering that other countries have fixated on Japan as a vital and lucrative market. Canada once exported raw materials to Japan relatively unchallenged; it is now encountering considerable competition from much more aggressive countries that are extremely anxious to do business. Between 1985 and 1991, New Zealand expanded its share of Japanese resource product imports at a higher rate than did Canada: imports of raw logs and timber jumped over 400 per cent, fish and seafood sales rose by more than 200 per cent, machinery and equipment sales increased by more than 650 per cent and imports of other manufactured items grew by almost 300 per cent. Australia experienced similar rapid growth in meat sales (more than 150 per cent) and food products (more than doubled). Both countries stand in stark contrast to Canada and its apparent inability to make headway in these markets. Even the United States, which is notorious for underestimating the cultural complexity of trade with Japan, more than doubled its exports of fish and seafood and increased its meat sales at an even faster pace (by almost 240 per cent). The importation of other foodstuffs from the United States grew at a rate of close to 500 per cent. The long-standing assumption that Japan blocks key export areas such as food and machinery to Western traders no longer holds. However, Canada has not yet adapted its trading approach to suit this new reality.

There is, perhaps, no threat greater than that from Japan's neighbours, the newly industrialized countries and the ASEAN nations (Association of South East Asian Nations), which are now competing with Canada for resource and manufactured products' market share and Japanese investment dollars. These countries offer many advantages, including low labour costs, environmental laws that are less stringent than those in North America and improvements in the quality of their manufactured products. As well, as the standard of living rises in countries from China to Indonesia, massive new consumer markets appear, promising great returns for companies that are ready to capitalize on new opportunities. Japanese business, understandably, is interested in these markets. What Canada must realize is that the gains these nations make in selling goods to Japan and securing Japanese investment may come partly at Canada's expense.

Japanese Society in Transition: Business Opportunities

Canadian business must also be aware that Japanese society is experiencing significant changes, which may present opportunities for new business ventures or presage shifts in spending or investment. For example, the percentage of Japan's population over the age of sixty-four is increasing more rapidly than that of the equivalent population in any other country. By the year 2020, this proportion will reach 22 per cent. (In the United States, which is also concerned about its changing demographics, this figure will rise to 16 per cent by the same year.) In the early 1980s, there were 8.5 Japanese workers for every retiree; by the year 2000, this number will drop to 2.5. These frightening statistics have resulted in changes: the age of mandatory retirement was recently raised from fifty-five to sixty and is likely to be increased to 65 in the near future. Seniors are being encouraged to work or volunteer.

This demographic shift will generate a need for goods and services designed for the elderly and will place inordinate pressures on the medical system, social services and pension plans. Traditionally, Japan has not had a very generous retirement system, and most elderly people moved in with their children when they were no longer self-sufficient. The crowded conditions in which most urban Japanese live make living as an extended family difficult, if not impossible. Powerful blocs of elderly Japanese will likely demand changes to Japan's meagre government pension plans just when the shrinking pool of workers is unable to pay for them.

The Japanese government has commissioned research on the prospect of establishing "silver cities" in other countries. These retirement villages would be completely Japanese in nature. The government wishes to give its seniors improved living conditions, away from the noise, crowding and pollution of large Japanese cities. With few such places left in Japan, attention is focusing on large, politically stable countries (Canada and Australia are prime candidates) that might be willing to accept an influx of aging, but self-supporting, Japanese. Canada may or may not wish to become involved in such ventures, but, depending on the arrangement negotiated, there could be some economic benefits to currently underpopulated regions of the country. Naturally, the best locations for such communities would have reasonably gentle climates and open space. Vancouver Island shows potential, but it is difficult to gauge how its residents, known for their opposition to continued development, would react to such an idea.

In a similar vein, the coming transformation of the Japanese work place presents some interesting scenarios for Canadian business. The Japanese, who currently work longer hours than any other national labour force, are under pressure from the government to cut back on the number of work hours. In June 1991, the Japanese Committee of Economic Councillors projected that the annual number of working hours will decrease from an average of 2,052 in 1990 to 1,700 by 2010. As working hours decline, Japanese workers will have much more leisure and travel time, and if there is no substantial drop in income, the market for everything from sports equipment to overseas holidays will grow considerably.

The Business of Education

Canadians have typically been loathe to talk of education (particularly at the postsecondary level) as an economic factor. For the last decade, however, large numbers of Asian young people have been coming to Canada to study. Recent figures from the Asia Pacific Foundation indicate that nearly 100,000 foreign students, the majority from Asia, study in Canada each year. These students contributed nearly $3 billion to the Canadian economy and supported 19,000 jobs. Students from Hong Kong and Taiwan come to upgrade their English language skills as rapidly as possible and then apply for admission into a Canadian university, sometimes first completing university transfer work at a community college. Singaporean students, who do not usually require English upgrading, take courses at the community college level and apply to university as transfer students. These students' native countries have a limited number of good universities, and the competition is staggering; second-tier students with the financial resources often opt for postsecondary education abroad.

Japanese students in Canada have different objectives. Most come only to study English, although big Japanese companies often send their brightest young employees to business administration programs in North America, usually at the best-known schools. While competition for the best universities in Japan is fierce, there is a plethora of middle-ranking universities and junior colleges, and the vast majority of Japanese would choose to attend one of these rather than a North American university. As mentioned previously, Japanese university life for students in fields other than medicine and engineering is a welcome break from the intense, focused life of studying that fills the high school years. Participating in clubs and making friends—contacts for the future—are more important than classes or assignments. Few Japanese would want to forego this hiatus for four much harder years at a North American university, to say nothing of the English language study that would be required for admission to a North American university.

Thousands of Japanese students study abroad each year, and most of them look for short-term (three to five week) English language and home-stay programs (in which students live in hosts' homes). In the past, institutions in Canada have approached this market in typical Canadian fashion—haphazardly and often in competition with each other. While there have been regional attempts at coordination, such as the British Columbia Centre for International Education, most Canadian colleges and universities have worked independently to attract foreign students. In 1994, the federal government and the Asia Pacific Foundation of Canada established a network of Canadian Education Centres in Asia, designed to coordinate the efforts of Canadian institutions. (This initiative will help the many Canadian schools that are trying to reduce overseas marketing activities due to budget cuts.) At issue, however, is whether or not colleges and universities will create strong, sustainable programs for Japanese students and others who are attracted to Canada. In several sectors of the education market, Canada has a clear advantage that has not yet been fully exploited.

Canadian Business and Japanese Markets

As mentioned previously, North American companies face numerous difficulties in attempting to penetrate the Japanese market. These challenges include complicated regulations regarding the importation of certain items: for example, it may still be required that pharmaceuticals be tested on Japanese subjects (subjects of any other ethnicity will not do) before being approved. And table napkins and tablecloths belong to different import categories, because napkins touch people's lips. In addition to these complexities, there is the multilayered distribution system, the emphasis on personal relationships and contacts, the need for a long-term commitment to the market and to customers, and the difficult Japanese language. For Canadian firms lacking the knowledge or experience to tackle these problems, the use of intermediaries or joint-venture partners may be the best route. An intermediary can not only help the Canadian company overcome these difficulties, but also give it access to Japanese industrial groups and foreign investors.

Canadians have responded half-heartedly to the increased importance of Japanese business and trade. There has been an upsurge of Canadian interest in foreign language and regional (i.e., Asian) studies. In British Columbia, many high schools offer classes in Mandarin and Japanese and enrolment in these areas at the postsecondary level has increased dramatically. Exchange programs and scholarships are available for students and teachers at both the secondary and postsecondary levels to study abroad, with certain programs targeting the Pacific Rim. However, it is not known if the skills and experiences gained during this time abroad are of interest to employers. In addition, the government, often the sponsor of exchanges and scholarships, offers no support in helping to convince employers of the benefits of hiring people with expertise in foreign language and area studies.

Government and business, both long on internationalist rhetoric and short on international action, must pay more attention to the training and employment of workers with language and cultural skills. Business often asserts that knowledge of Asian languages and cultures, while valuable, must be combined with other skills—that is, that this knowledge is not a valuable, marketable skill in its own right. Due to the complexity of Asian writing systems, mastery to any reasonable degree usually takes longer than for most Romance languages (four years of full-time study is an often-cited guideline).

Moreover, students desiring any level of cultural understanding must spend at least a year in the country in question. Requiring students to have Asian language and culture skills, plus a law, business or forestry degree, is a tall order. Nonetheless, if industry and business made its requirements more clearly known, and placed a premium on hiring people with cultural skills, students would make the necessary personal sacrifices. Students who have invested over five years in learning about Japanese culture and society are reluctant to take positions that do not utilize these abilities. Without efforts to tie Asian language and culture skills and job opportunities, the funding for scholarships and exchanges is partly wasted.

The active recruitment of people with language and culture expertise into the business world is very limited. Although Canadian companies profess an interest in recruiting Asia Pacific specialists, they seldom hire them. Most companies prefer to hire interpreters, translators or consultants on contract; many North American firms continue the bravado of the past, forging ahead without anyone on staff with knowledge of the country in question. Consultants hired on contract often lack a thorough understanding of the company's product, personnel, service or corporate culture. In addition, reliance on outside consultants means that the company does not benefit from an accumulation of knowledge about the society and business culture of its customers.

Recently, crash courses in languages and business culture have started to appear. These classes are based on the premise that senior personnel who need some language skills can learn the basics in a couple of six-week sets of lessons. In fact, most of these business people are too busy to devote the time and energy necessary to make much progress in the language. The knowledge gained from four years of full-time study cannot be acquired in such a short time. Seminars on Japanese business practices, commercial etiquette and business opportunities provide only the barest introduction and cannot substitute for a substantial commitment to cross-cultural understanding. The classes offer an appropriate way for business people to gain the tools that will make them more comfortable and more effective in Japan, China or Korea, but they do not substitute for the skills of a specialist.

In contrast, Japanese firms and government agencies make a concerted effort to understand North American conditions and cultures. Most Japanese companies keep a careful watch on North America, maintaining newspaper-clipping services and carefully following the nuances of Canadian and American developments. It is difficult to imagine a Canadian firm paying such close attention to the details of Japanese society and politics; most maintain only a perfunctory knowledge of Japan.

Canadians seem to be content with half measures, with reaching forward without actually taking a step. This tendency, perhaps more than any other characteristic, indicates how far Canada has to go to become a true trading nation. Too often, Canadian companies that hire area specialists offer these employees almost no chance to use their skills; they end up working on completely unrelated tasks. In other cases, managers ask for advice but are reluctant to follow it. "Must we do things their way?" is a common lament. One large Canadian tourism-related company advertised for Japanese speakers, but the language tests they administered to prospective employees were so basic that many of the thirty people they hired could barely make themselves understood in the language. When the time came to decide which of the new employees would work most frequently with the Japanese customers, the employees drew lots. As it turned out, those with the best Japanese language skills had the worst luck and seldom saw Japanese customers.

Examples like this illustrate the limited commitment of Canadians and Canadian companies to even the simplest cross-cultural gesture in their efforts to penetrate the Japanese market. A recently published study of the implications of Japanese economic policies for businesses in Canada states that "investments in cultural and linguistic education to increase the understanding of Japanese ways and tastes and the ability to communicate in Japanese are essential for developing and maintaining Canadian skills for exporting to Japan. Canadian government leadership is needed in these areas" (Nakamura and Vertinsky, *Japanese Economic Policies and Growth*, p. 204). Observers have been saying for years that Canadian business must gain a greater understanding of Japanese social and business culture and use that knowledge as the basis for long-term financial and organizational commitments. However, Canadians have ignored this suggestion. If Canada continues to assign a low priority to gaining this understanding, the adverse effects will be felt for a long time.

There is only a smattering of evidence that Canadian companies are prepared to make a significant and long-term commitment to organizing their internal operations and thus capitalize on the Japanese market. Instead, continuing a long-established Canadian pattern, Canadian business responds primarily to short-term opportunities and relies on contract specialists to interpret the nuances of the Japanese business culture. Given the unique nature of Japan and its commercial world, half-hearted measures will not suffice in the long term.

Canada, still struggling to catch up with the changes of the past decade, must now come to terms with the transitions in the Japanese economy. If the yen continues to trade near its current level, Japan will again be faced with a need for economic restructuring, as it was a decade ago. This restructuring will likely mean a greater emphasis on high technology and elimination of the frills on Japanese products. Auto industry analysts refer to the latter strategy as " 'de-contenting'— taking out things consumers won't notice and won't miss." As it has become increasingly difficult for Japanese automakers to produce affordable cars, they are de-contenting by leaving parts that cannot be seen unpainted and by eliminating some of the luxury items. For Canada, the increased value of the yen should make Canadian products more competitive vis-a-vis Japanese products; however, the two countries compete in very few product categories. Canada does import a sizeable variety and quantity of products from Japan, and for importers, the rapid rise of the yen could be quite traumatic. Ultimately, though, consumers will pay most dearly.

As Japan struggles with the implications of the changing value of the yen, it will have to consider increasing offshore manufacturing to take advantage of lower labour costs. Although many countries are interested in Japan's capital, Canada offers distinct advantages: a stable, well-educated workforce at reasonable rates (given the weakness of the Canadian dollar), a market of 30 million people in one of the world's most affluent countries and relatively easy access, as a result of the Canada–United States Free Trade Agreement and NAFTA, to the huge American market. Canada has low energy costs, abundant resources and government-financed medical and pension programs. In addition, the country offers high-quality research and development establishments and a relatively calm political and social environment, without the aggressive nationalism or anti-Japanese sentiment present in many other nations.

Does Canada wish to be the future recipient of Japanese investment money? If so, the country must decide which sectors and which parts of the country will benefit and specify the conditions under which these investments will be made. Canada must determine what it has to sell and what it wants in return. If Canada does not volunteer suggestions, the decision of whether or not to invest in Canada will fall solely on Japan. If Japan does invest, the choice of targets of investment will result from a series of individual decisions without broad Canadian input, similar to the way in which Japanese business became involved in northern British Columbia. So far, Canada's approach can be summarized as haphazard, short-term, product-based and not particularly culturally sensitive. It is time for the country to be more accountable for its decisions. The responsibility rests with Canadians and the Canadian government to determine what is best, economically and socially, for the country—and to fulfil those requirements. Canada may decide it does not want increased Japanese investment. Whatever the decision, Canada must clearly assert its position, rather than simply letting events unfold.

Canada has two choices: it can continue down the path toward greater continental integration through NAFTA or it can seek to establish long-term, stable markets in other countries. If it chooses to try new markets, Japan is an obvious target; a decades-long tradition of trade with Japan, established Japanese markets for Canadian raw materials and the multitude of opportunities for value-added and manufacturing sales in the "new" Japan have set up the preconditions for success. Japan's wealthy corporations have also shown their willingness and ability to capitalize on Canadian investment opportunities. However, Canada must decide if the long-entrenched pattern of foreign ownership of key resource sectors remains in the country's best interests.

What, then, are the prospects for meaningful and systematic change? Realistically, they are minimal. Canada's complex, competitive political and commercial structures limit the chances of a coordinated response, much as the country's well-established tradition of following the easiest and more obvious trade opportunities reduces the likelihood of a concerted effort towards enhancing Japanese trade. The intricacies of government in Canada—a retreating federal government competing with assertive provinces and territories—seriously interfere with the country's ability to make coherent, systematic and long-term commitments to business opportunities. Furthermore, the corporate culture in Canada, strongly controlled by multinationals and long protected by Canadian tariffs, is far from innovative, creative or forward looking. Although the business community in Canada is quick to criticize the government for its inaction on economic matters, Canadian companies do not have a strong international reputation for responsiveness, cultural sensitivity or long-term planning.

The emphasis on trade delegations, designed as much for domestic political consumption as for the establishment of long-term commercial relations, masks the need for coordinated, nationwide corporate and department-level efforts to capitalize on Japanese markets. Given this reality, the development of an appropriate response will likely fall to the regional/provincial level. Individual provinces or parts of provinces, whether they decide to target Japanese business opportunities or wish to discourage Japanese investment, might be better able to capitalize on the situation. Again, however, there is little indication that this will occur and limited likelihood of any region or province developing a systematic approach to Japanese opportunities.

***

Japan will continue to figure prominently in Canadian trade and direct foreign investment in Canada. Recent trends indicate that Canada's business relationship with Japan is stagnating, restricted to exporting resources to Japan and providing a base for Japanese companies interested in manufacturing for the American market, at a time when Japan is facing massive internal social, economic and political transitions. It is commonplace for Canada to rely on the quality and price of its raw materials, and the dependability of its supply, to ensure its attractiveness to lucrative international markets. However, in the globalized markets of the twenty-first century, this *laissez-faire*, haphazard approach may be inappropriate. To prosper as an international trading nation and become more than an economic satellite of the United States (a not altogether unpalatable option that has made this country wealthy and economically stable), Canada must assume a more internationalist perspective and make the effort to learn more about its foreign trading partners. The country would do well to begin with Japan.

10

Approaching the
Twenty-First Century

I think Canadians have very friendly feelings for Japan and
Japan-Canada relations are quite good. I also think that much
can be done to strengthen the relationship because Canadians
are now somewhat engrossed in internal politics. Japan is also
undergoing great change. We are debating internally where we
go from here now that Japan is an economic power. We are
debating Japan's future role in the world. In spite of the friendly
relations between Japan and Canada there is still a lack of
understanding between us. My feeling is that relations between
Canada and Japan are in good shape, but there is a lot that has
to be done.

—H.E. Michio Mizoguchi,
Japan's Ambassador to Canada,
August 1992 (Canada-Japan Trade Council,
Newsletter, 1992)

As the twenty-first century approaches, the pace and complexity of
contemporary issues challenge individual nations and the global
community. The world faces technological, demographic, environmental, economic and cultural transformations on a massive scale.
Nationalism and its attendant ethnic rivalries run rampant in the
states of the former Soviet Union, in the former Yugoslavia, in
Rwanda and in Cambodia. Communism and socialism have fallen
into disrepute around the globe; even the People's Republic of China
has succumbed to the enticements of industry and prosperity. But the
consequences of a world dominated by capitalism are yet to be fully
realized. The effects of the ecological destruction that humankind
has wrought on the planet appear in all corners of the world, sparking
predictions of global catastrophe by doomsayers.

As the world changes, so must its constituent parts, either enthusiastically by embracing the new internationalism or grudgingly by
bowing to the pressures of a globalized economy, ecology and culture. Canada and Japan, two of the world's richest nations, find
themselves enveloped in the maelstrom of the contemporary transformation. Neither country may be happy with all of the consequences, such as the growing impact of American mass culture (the
same Michael Jordan T-shirt that is popular in rural British Columbia
is a big seller in downtown Tokyo), but both recognize that major
shifts are underway. In other transformations—for example, the deterioration of the world's ecosystem—Canada and Japan are com-
plicit, for they are both heavy consumers of resources, and neither
has a particularly glowing reputation for placing the protection of the
planet ahead of short-term prosperity. Canada and Japan find themselves struggling, in very different ways, to find the political vision
and national will necessary to cope with the new realities; both are
finding their current leadership to be seriously wanting in the skills
and foresight needed to guide their nations toward an uncertain
future.

Despite their problems, Canada and Japan remain at or near the
top of the list of the world's nations when judged on their standards
of living. In the UN rankings of the "best countries" in the world in
which to live, Canada and Japan are consistently in the top three,
blessed with good health care and education, long life expectancy,
comparative equality of circumstance and improving opportunities
for women. Both countries have their weak spots. In Canada, the gap
between rich and poor is widening, concerns about budgetary deficits
and debt grow and the sustainability of the resource-dependent economy is questionable. In Japan, the lack of affordable decent housing
in crowded cities and the high levels of pollution diminish the attractiveness of the country for some of its residents. Nonetheless, Canada
and Japan are two of the world's richest, most stable and most
peaceful countries. Few nations in the world would hesitate to swap
problems with either Japan or Canada.

Canada and Japan are, of course, far from similar. Their histories,
core values, social systems, and economic and political structures
vary greatly. However, while they have had very different pasts, their
futures hold many of the same challenges. How each nation reacts
will be largely determined by their core values and cultural assumptions. Responses to opportunities and problems do not emerge in a
vacuum; instead, they develop from, and reflect, the underlying ide-

als, expectations and understanding of individual cultures. The future, then, is conditioned by the past, and a nation's reactions to change fall within the range of behaviours established over time.

As Canada and Japan prepare themselves for the future, the national governments face the delicate task of balancing the general health of the nation with the needs and aspirations of its individual citizens. This dilemma highlights the most striking difference between Canada and Japan. Since the end of World War II, Japan has been preoccupied with the "big picture" of economic growth and increased national prosperity. The overriding focus of both the Japanese government and the Japanese citizenry has been the good of the nation: catching up with the West in industrial terms, rebuilding Japan, strengthening the economy and gaining influence on the international stage. During this same period, Canada has directed much of its political and public energy toward improving the material conditions of its citizens, expanding the rights and freedoms of individuals, and, most importantly, responding to the specific demands of interest groups, ethnic minorities and regions (what J.M.S. Careless has referred to as Canada's "limited identities"—the subgroups that typically gain an allegiance stonger than that to the nation state).

Serious questions remain unanswered. Has Canada, in elevating the status of individual rights, made the correct choice? Will it be able to mount the national campaigns necessary to rally the nation for the next century? Has Japan, in demanding allegiance from its citizens in building the foundation of a strong, international economy, positioned itself properly for the social and economic turmoil of the coming decades? More pointedly, will the current and future generations of Japanese citizens make the same commitment to national success that their ancestors did, and will it be sufficient to overcome the nation's problems and meet pressing social needs?

As Canada and Japan set out to address the conflicts between the "big picture" problems of the national economy and the aspirations of individuals, they will find their options limited, if not determined, by culture and history. What is possible in Japan is not necessarily possible in Canada, and vice versa. Which nation—a homogeneous one, with a dominant ethnicity and broadly shared values, or a heterogeneous one, with complex ethnic composition and few shared values—is better equipped to respond to the economic and social conditions of this generation? The answer does not appear to favour Canada.

Although the discussion of Canada's future is rarely framed in terms of the national perspective versus individual prosperity, governments have been leading the country in this direction. The reforms of the Klein government in Alberta, which focus on deficit reduction and which are not favourably disposed toward welfare recipients, are now being mirrored in Ontario and by the federal government. The country's growing interest in international trading blocks (including the decision, which would have sparked endless controversy only a few years ago, to separate Canada's economic interests from campaigns to promote human rights in other countries), the signing of NAFTA, the high (human) costs of keeping inflation in check and the current preoccupation with debt are all manifestations of the victory of the "big picture" over the interests of individuals and economic equity.

Canada is facing a considerable problem with its burgeoning debt, which is currently close to $500 billion and growing by close to $30 billion annually (not including provincial debts). Despite Canada's recent "tough" budget, the debt will continue to grow and efforts to contain it will cause increasing personal hardship over the next five to ten years, unless the Liberal government surrenders to the inevitable protests and returns to its individualistic agenda. Canada should also have concerns about its overdependence on the sale of natural resources. The vast majority of Canada's exports are resource products, and politicians and the general public are only now awakening to the frightening reality that resources are finite. The cod fishery in Newfoundland has been closed because of depleted fish stocks; forestry companies in northern British Columbia are going as far as Manitoba and the Yukon in search of trees; and debate rages with the United States over the future of the North Pacific salmon stocks. These resource depletions have environmental, social and economic implications, and Canada must make some serious choices about the future direction of its economy.

Perhaps the major economic decision has already been made. Canada has allowed itself to become particularly dependent on the United States. Despite its rhetoric of international commerce, Canada has become increasingly continental in its trade. Over three-quarters of the country's exports currently have American destinations, and 65 per cent of imports originate there. The United States is the source of about 64 per cent of Canada's foreign direct investment and the recipient of 63 per cent of Canada's direct investment abroad. Few countries in the world have tied their future as tightly to the economy of another single nation; no other country is as seemingly oblivious to the consequences—positive and negative—of this action.

Japan faces challenges in the economic sphere, but they are of a different nature. The changing value of the yen is forcing Japanese exporters to again consider strategies for coping with the escalating costs of their products. There have been crises in the financial sector, new challenges for exporting companies, and economic slow-down in Japan itself. Likely solutions for these problems include an increase in overseas manufacturing, "de-contenting" of exports to Western countries, and an increased emphasis on high-technology products. Japan's relationship with the United States is another troubling area. For over a decade, relations between these powerful trading partners have been strained, due to Japan's sizeable trade surplus. The United States maintains that Japan must do more to open its markets and encourage the purchase of American goods; thus continues the American tradition of blaming Japan for the commercial and economic failings of the United States. Despite talk of a severe Japanese recession, Japan jumped from sixth to second in income per capita between 1989 and 1993, unemployment in 1994 stood at around 3 per cent, inflation was less than 1 per cent, and not a single significant employer collapsed. Economically crippled by a lost war only fifty years ago, the country had, by 1993, created an economy that was 68 per cent of the size of the United States' and that could challenge America as the nation with the world's largest economy by the turn of the century.

Japan, unlike Canada, is currently balancing tangible economic options. The country has been actively involved with the rapid expansion of the Southeast Asian economies, which are currently growing at 6 to 7 per cent per year and expected to continue to expand at this rate into the next century. Japan currently channels close to half of its direct foreign investment into the United States, but increasing trade difficulties and the weakening of the North American economy have convinced many Japanese corporations to direct their new investments to Asia. East Asia now attracts about 15 per cent of Japan's investment; within a decade or so, the value of Japan's involvement in the region will increase to close to 40 per cent, mostly at North America's expense. Canada's profile is not distinct from that of the United States; for example, major investments in automobile manufacturing are designed for both the American and Canadian markets. Because of this situation, Japan's reorientation will have a strong impact on Canada as well. Japan can, and likely will, have a prosperous future with a declining emphasis on the United States and Canada.

As individuals, the Japanese and Canadians are probably as healthy and contented as the people of any other nation; this contentment is easily recognizable among the proud Japanese but only rarely seen among the more cynical and self-critical Canadians. From all indications, most Japanese feel themselves to be an integral part of society and are not unhappy with their lives. While Japan is a highly structured, consensus-oriented society, there is surprising openness and considerable public dissent; Japan has an extremely open press, although the major newspapers follow the nationalist line closely.

There are problems, though, for those who do not belong or feel they belong to the "Japanese Club." As described earlier, these outsiders include youth whose needs are not met by the rigid education system, women who do not wish to choose between career and marriage, the *burakumin*, the Koreans, the Ainu, foreign workers and average Japanese who march to the beat of a slightly different drummer. For these people, Japan leaves something to be desired. But while no country can satisfy all of its citizens, Japan comes closer than most.

Most of Canada's citizens, if pressed, would also profess to being happy to be Canadians. Canada provides considerable freedom and individual choice; the country imposes few of the limitations on behaviour, thought and aspirations that exist within Japan. Canada's multiculturalism and liberalism, while not without flaws, allow Canadians to live pretty much as they wish. To a degree that Canadian social critics rarely admit, there is remarkable acceptance of differences, both legally and socially. Canadians make numerous accommodations for differences: buildings are accessible for people in wheelchairs, dress codes have been removed from schools (in a recent case in British Columbia, a high school student demanded that he be permitted to wear a dress to school), some provinces provide benefits for same-sex couples, the Charter of Rights protects individual rights and national programs permit individuals considerable flexibility in pursuing their personal goals. Canadians can now work out of their homes, return to school as adults and change careers numerous times. And employment is based on ability, not gender, race or religion (although the situation is far from perfect).

These accommodations are extremely positive, but, cumulatively, they have come at a price. Liberty and licence are not free; they present both financial and social costs for the nation. Individuals and groups have pushed so hard for their own agendas that they have missed the larger picture. Trade unions, business groups, regional promoters, libertarians, anti–gun control campaigners and countless special interest groups want their demands satisfied immediately. There has been little willingness to cooperate, to compromise, to work toward the common good or to suspend personal gratification in the interest of the nation. In short, the Canadian "team" has not pulled together, and Canadian governments have relied on decades of prosperity and the artificial confidence of debt-financed programs to paper over the differences. The result is that the country has an enormous debt and a rocky economy. The near future, while not bleak, comes with scarce funds. There is no longer adequate money for health care and education in some parts of the country, let alone funding for multicultural programs and special interest concerns. Trying to please everyone has left no one pleased, many decisions remain to be made (aboriginal land claims are only just being dealt with) and governments find their coffers empty and the public intolerant of additional taxation.

The contrast between Canada and Japan on this issue of the nation versus the individual is striking. Japan does not hesitate to place the needs of the group ahead of those of the individual and expects its citizens to accept this stance as the national standard. Canada has moved away from a strong commitment to group rights and collective responsibility and is advancing, many would say too quickly, toward the deification of individual rights and personal responsibility and a consequent sharp reduction in the role of government. The implications of these national differences will become very significant as Canada and Japan attempt to come to terms with the many social and economic problems of the twenty-first century.

Perhaps these two countries could learn from one another. It may be that the right way to balance the big picture and individual needs is neither Japan's way nor Canada's way, but a combination of both. Japan's success suggests that only by putting the nation's health first will governments achieve the economic success required to allow their citizens more choice, more freedom and more of the "good things" in life. Canada's approach worked in the short term, and provided the country's citizens with an enviable level of prosperity, but as recent financial difficulties make clear, a reliance on government funding (particularly when a great deal of the money is borrowed) does not provide a long-term solution.

Canada's heterogeneity means that it would be impossible to evoke the degree of national focus and commitment that is evident in Japan. However, it is vital that Canada at least begin to look toward the future and examine what is good for the country as a whole. Japan does not have all of the answers, but it has some; Canadians would do well to observe and learn. As one writer recently commented, "Many of the world's problems boil down to requiring today's generation to make sacrifices to ensure a more secure future for future generations. That is a tough choice for a Western democracy, but it is one that Confucianism instinctively approaches with the right mindset." (Eamonn Finkleton, *Blindside*, p. 352). Canada illustrates how Western liberalism and individualism establish a short-term orientation and limit the prospects for a collective response. The country had the right mind set for the first fifty years after World War II; as Japan and the Canada-Japan relationship reveal, Canada likely has not adopted the appropriate approach for the next century. Given what is at stake—the economic prosperity and social stability of the nation—it is imperative that Canada learn from other countries and begin the necessary but potentially painful process of preparing itself for the new global realities.

Guide to Further Reading

There is a vast literature on Japanese history and contemporary Japan. The following provides a guide to recent writing on Japan and Canada-Japan relations; it seeks to be suggestive rather than exhaustive.

Understanding Japan

There are a handful of excellent and interesting books that will help an outsider come to terms with Japan. The standard introduction is Edwin Reischauer, *The Japanese Today: Change and Continuity* (London: Harvard University Press, 1988); this should be followed by Karel van Wolferen's interesting *The Enigma of Japanese Power* (Toronto: Macmillan, 1990), *The Japanese* (New York: E.P. Dutton, 1987) by Peter Tasker and Joy Hendry, and *Understanding Japanese Society* (London: Routledge, 1987). From here, an understanding of Japanese history is essential. Richard Storry, *A History of Modern Japan* (Toronto: Penguin, 1982) provides an introduction, as does W.G. Beasley, *The Rise of Modern Japan: Political, Economic and Social Change since 1850* (London: Weidenfeld, 1995). *Postwar Japan as History* (Los Angeles: University of California Press, 1993), edited by Andrew Gorden, provides a thorough introduction to this period. Also informative is Hugh Cortazzi, *Modern Japan: A Concise Survey* (London: Macmillan, 1993) and John Condon, *With Respect to the Japanese: A Guide for Americans* (Yarmouth: Intercultural Press, 1984).

For a critical review of the Japanese education system, see Ken Schoolland, *Shogun's Ghost: The Dark Side of Japanese Education* (New York: Bergin and Garvey, 1990). On the more contemporary scene, see Jared Taylor, *Shadows of the Rising Sun: A Critical View of the "Japanese Miracle"* (Tokyo: Tuttle, 1983), Steven Reed, *Making Common Sense of Japan* (Pittsburg: University of Pittsburg Press, 1993), Eyal Ben-Ari et al., *Unwrapping Japan* (Honolulu: University of Hawaii Press, 1990). For perspectives on "everyday" life in Japan, see Donald Richie, *Geisha, Gangster, Neighbour, Nun: Scenes from Japanese Lives* (Tokyo: Kodansha International, 1987), Norma Field, *In the Realm of a Dying Emperor: Japan at Century's*

End (New York: Vintage, 1993), Robert Christopher, *The Japanese Mind* (New York: Fawcett Columbine, 1983), David Mura, *Turning Japanese: Memories of a Sansei* (New York: Anchor, 1991), Joe Joseph, *The Japanese: Strange but Not Strangers* (London: Penguin, 1994). Of a more academic nature are Joseph Tobin, ed., *Re-Made in Japan: Everyday Life and Consumer Taste in a Changing Society* (New Haven: Yale University Press, 1992) and Peter Dale, *The Myth of Japanese Uniqueness* (London: Routledge, 1986). For an excellent recent study of the "underside" of Japanese society, see Karl Greenfeld, *Speed Tribes: Days and Nights with Japan's Next Generation* (New York: HarperCollins, 1994).

Japanese Business

One of the best books for placing Japan's business culture in context is Charles Hampden-Turner and Alfons Trompenaars's, *The Seven Cultures of Capitalism* (Toronto: Doubleday, 1993). *Taking Japan Seriously: A Confucian Perspective on Leading Economic Issues* (London: Athlone, 1987), by Ronald Dore, offers an important cultural angle on Japanese business. For a uniquely accessible introduction to the Japanese economy, see Shotaro Ishinomori, *Japan Inc: Introduction to Japanese Economics* (Los Angeles: University of California Press, 1988). An excellent study on postwar developments is Shigeto Tsuru's *Japan's Capitalism: Creative Defeat and Beyond* (Cambridge: Cambridge University Press, 1993). For an overview of the Japanese economic system, see Takatoshi Ito, *The Japanese Economy* (Cambridge, Mass.: MIT Press, 1992). Particularly useful on Japan-U.S.A. trade is Ryuzo Sato's *The Chrysanthemum and the Eagle* (New York: New York University Press, 1994). See also Mark Zimmerman, *How to do Business with the Japanese* (Tokyo: Tuttle, 1985) and Micahel Czinkota and Jon Woronoff, *Unlocking Japan's Markets: Seizing Marketing and Distribution Opportunities in Today's Japan* (Tokyo: Tuttle, 1993).

On the Japanese corporate world, see James Abegglen and George Stalk, Jr., *Kaisha: The Japanese Corporation* (New York: Basic Books, 1985) and Bill Emmott, *Japan's Global Reach: The Influences, Strategies and Weaknesses of Japan's Multinational Companies* (New York: Arrow, 1993). For an excellent analytical study, see Mashiko Aoki and Ronald Dore, eds., *The Japanese Firm: Sources of Competitive Strength* (Oxford: Claredon Press, 1994). Also useful is Arthur Whitehill, *Japanese Management* (London: Routledge, 1990). If any indication is needed as to why America, in its occasionally stultifying arrogance, has difficulty understanding Japan, read (but do not buy) one of the most irritating books on Japan published in recent years: Ray and Cindelyn Eberts, *The Myths of Japanese Quality* (New Jersey: Prentice Hall, 1995).

There are several excellent studies of Japan's role within the Asia Pacific region. See James Fallows, *Looking at the Sun: The Rise of the New East Asian Economic and Political System* (New York: Vintage, 1995) and James Abegglen, *Sea Change: Pacific Asia as the New World Industrial Centre* (Toronto: Free Press, 1994). Japan has, in recent years, moved to the forefront of commercial innovation. The best study of this is Ikujiro Nonaka and Hirotaka Takeuchi's, *The Knowledge Creating Company: How Japanese Companies Created the Dynamics of Innovation* (New York: Oxford University Press, 1995). For a light look at new developments, see Leonard Koren, *283 Useful Ideas from Japan* (San Francisco: Chronicle Books, 1988). On Japanese consumer behaviour, see George Fields, *From Bonsai to Levis* (New York: Signet, 1985) and his *Gucci on the Ginza: Japan's New Consumer Generation* (New York: Kodansha International, 1989).

Japan's Future

There is a vast and confusing array of literature on Japan's future, ranging from the wildly optimistic to the seriously pessimistic. For a fascinating Japanese perspective, see Ichiro Ozawa, *Blueprint for a New Japan: The Rethinking of a Nation* (New York: Kodansha International, 1994). Also provocative is Shintaro Ishihara, *The Japan That Can Say No: Why Japan Will Be First among Equals* (Toronto: Touchstone, 1989). *Japan: A New Kind of Superpower* (Baltimore: Johns Hopkins University Press, 1994), edited by Craig Garby and Mary Brown Bullock, provides a scholarly analysis of the country's changing international role. One of the most provocative books in the field, is Eamonn Fingleton's *Blindside: Why Japan Is Still on Track to Overtake the U.S. by the Year 2000* (Boston: Houghton Mifflin, 1995).

Canada-Japan Relations

While there are relatively few books on Canada-Japan relations, there are some useful studies. For a good introduction to several aspects of Canadian-Japanese relations, see John Schultz and Kimitada Miwa, *Canada and Japan in the Twentieth Century* (Toronto: Oxford University Press, 1991). One of the best books, particularly for business people, is editor Jane Withey's *Doing Business in Japan: An Insider's Guide* (Toronto: Key Porter, 1994). Also useful is Klaus Pringsheim's *Neighbours across the Pacific: The Development of Economic and Political Relations Between Canada and Japan* (Westport: Greenwood Press, 1983) and Richard Wright, *Japanese Business in Canada: The Elusive Alliance* (Montreal: Institute for Research on Public Policy, 1984). For a biography of a Canadian missionary/activist in Japan, see Margaret Prang, *A Heart at Leisure from Itself: Caroline Macdonald* (Vancouver: UBC Press, 1995). On Canadian foreign policy, see Norman Hillmer and J.L. Granatstein, *Empire to Umpire: Canada and the World to the 1990s* (Toronto: Copp Clark Longman, 1994).

A thorough study, from a Canadian perspective, of Japanese economic activities related to North America, is Masao Nakamura and Ilan Vertinsky's *Japanese Economic Policies and Growth: Implications for Businesses in Canada and North America* (Edmonton: University of Alberta Press, 1994). *The Last Great Forest: Japanese Multinationals and Alberta's Northern Forests* (Edmonton: NewWest Press, 1994), by Larry Pratt and Ian Urquhart, provides an excellent case study of Japanese forest development. Also very useful is David Edginton's *Japanese Direct Investment in Canada: Recent Trends and Prospects* (Vancouver: UBC Dept. of Geography, 1992) and Frank Langdon, *The Politics of Canadian-Japanese Economic Relations, 1952–1983* (Vancouver: UBC Press, 1983). See also R. Stern, *Trade and Investment Relations among the United States, Canada, and Japan* (Chicago: University of Chicago Press, 1989).

On the experience of Japanese immigrants and Japanese Canadians, see the excellent novels by Joy Kogawa, *Obasan* (Toronto: Penguin, 1983) and *Itsuka* (Toronto: Penguin, 1993), Ken Adachi, *The Enemy That Never Was: A History of the Japanese-Canadians* (Toronto: McClelland and Stewart, 1976), Ann Gomer Sunahara, *The Politics of Racism: The Uprooting of Japanese Canadians during the Second World War* (Toronto: James Lorimer, 1981), Patricia Roy, *A White Man's Province* (Vancouver: UBC Press, 1991), Peter Ward, *White Canada Forever* (Montreal: McGill-Queen's University Press, 1994). The best study of World War II is Pat Roy et al., *Mutual Hostages: Canadians and Japanese during the Second World War* (Toronto: University of Toronto Press, 1990).

Index

ABC Nishihawa, 143
Aclo Compounders, 144
Ainu, 79, 173
Alberta-Pacific, 141
Alcan Aluminum, 123-4, 149
Alcan Smelters and Chemicals, 123
Aleutian Islands, 41
aluminum, 123-4
Amada Promecam, 144
Amaterasu, 16
Anglo-Japanese Alliance, 22, 31
anti-Japanese riot. *See* Vancouver Riot of 1907
antiforeigner mobs, 32
Aoki, 146
artisans, 17
ASEAN (Association of South East Asian Nations), 159. *See also* Southeast Asia
Asia Pacific Foundation, 63, 123, 160, 161
Asia Pacific specialists, 163, 164
Asiatic Exclusion League, 27
atomic bomb, 46
Atoms International, 143
Australia, 1, 3, 8, 113, 119, 147, 158
Automobiles: and Japan-U.S. trade relations, 104, 115; Japanese, 112; Japanese automakers and new Asian markets, 116, 172. *See also* offshore manufacturing
Autopact, 142

Bank of Japan, 87
banks, Japanese, 145-7
Bellemar Parts, 143
Birchall, L.J., 42
Bougie, Jacques, 123
Bridgestone, 143
Britain, 7, 32, 56, 106, 133, 135
British Columbia: aluminum, 123; coal, 118-22; fish and seafood, 122; lumber, 118-9; pine mushrooms, 124-6
British Columbia Centre for International Education, 161
British Commonwealth Air Training Plan, 39
Brunei, 117
Bullmoose mines, 121

burakumin (untouchables), 79, 173
business culture, 85-103

CAMI Automotive, 142, 144
Can. Auto Parts, 143
Canada: access to American market, 157-8, 165; business and government, 89-90; economy, 6, 13, 104, 105, 114; future challenges, 170-1; geography, 4-5; Japanese image of, 2, 157-8; Japanese investments in, 1-2, 132-47, 150-2, 157-8, 172; multiculturalism and liberalism, 173-5; North American continentalism, 57, 60, 166, 171; population, 4; postwar relations with Japan, 58-63; public debt, 169, 171; and World War II, 38-42
Canada Mold Tech., 144
Canada Packers, 149
Canada-Japan Business Cooperation Council, 123
Canada-Japan Businessmen's Conference, 62
Canada-Japan Forum 2000, 62
Canada-Japan trade: to 1950s, 105-10; 1950s-1985, 35, 110-2; Plaza Accord and, 112-3; in mid-1990s, 13-4, 114-7; future of, 153-67, 168; Canadian exports, 2, 3, 117-26; Japanese exports, 126-30; relationship, 104-5. *See also* Framework for Economic Cooperation; trading relationships
Canada-Japan Trade Council, 60
Canada-United States Free Trade Agreement, 105
Canadian Airlines International, 149
Canadian Army Pacific Command, 45
Canadian Bank Act, 145
Canadian business culture, 101-2, 166
Canadian Chopstick Manufacturing Company, 141-2
Canadian Education Centres, 161
Canadian exports: manufactured goods, 107, 113; raw and semiprocessed materials, 113-4
Canadian Pacific Railway, 26
Canadian Studies programs, 4, 61

• Cap-Saint-Ignace
• Sainte-Marie (Beauce)
Québec, Canada
1996

« L'IMPRIMEUR »